TECHNIQUES OF
FAMILY PSYCHOTHERAPY

A Primer

Seminars in Psychiatry

TECHNIQUES OF FAMILY PSYCHOTHERAPY

A Primer

Edited by

Donald A. Bloch, M.D.

Director
Nathan W. Ackerman Family Institute
New York

GRUNE & STRATTON
A Subsidiary of Harcourt Brace Jovanovich, Publishers
NEW YORK AND LONDON

Techniques of Family Psychotherapy: A Primer is reprinted from the May 1973 issue (Volume V, Number 2) of the quarterly journal *Seminars in Psychiatry*, published by Grune & Stratton, Inc.

Library of Congress Cataloging in Publication Data

Main entry under title:

Techniques of family psychotherapy.

   "Reprinted from the May 1973 issue (volume 5, number 2) of the quarterly journal Seminars in psychiatry."
   Includes bibliographical references.
   1. Family psychotherapy.   I. Bloch, Donald A., ed.   II. Seminars in psychiatry.   [DNLM: 1. Family therapy.   WM 430 B651t   1973]
RC488.5.T4   616.8'915   73-6655
ISBN 0-8089-0818-9

©1973 by Grune & Stratton, Inc.

Grune & Stratton, Inc.
111 Fifth Avenue, New York, New York 10003

Library of Congress Catalog Card Number 73-6655
International Standard Book Number 0-8089-0818-9

Printed in the United States of America

Contributors

Alger, Ian, M.D., Clinical Assistant Professor of Psychiatry and Training Analyst, New York Medical College, and Senior Research Associate, Center for Policy Research, New York, N.Y.

Bloch, Donald A., M.D., Director, Nathan W. Ackerman Family Institute, New York, N.Y.

Duhl, Bunny S., B.A., Instructor, Boston Family Institute and Center for Training in Family Therapy, Boston State Hospital, Boston, Mass.

Duhl, Frederick J., M.D., Director of Training, Boston Family Institute; Director of Education, Boston State Hospital; and Assistant Professor of Psychiatry, Tufts University Medical School, Boston, Mass.

Framo, James L., Ph.D., Chief, Family Therapy and Training Unit, Jefferson Community Mental Health Center, Department of Psychiatry, Thomas Jefferson University, Philadelphia, Pa.

Franklin, Paul, M.D., Supervising psychiatrist and faculty member, Nathan W. Ackerman Family Institute, New York, N.Y.

Kantor, David, Ph.D., Director of Research, Boston Family Institute; Director of Psychological Research, Boston State Hospital; and Assistant Professor of Psychology, Tufts University Medical School, Boston, Mass.

LaPerriere, Kitty, Ph.D., Director of Education, Nathan W. Ackerman Family Institute, New York, N.Y.

Laqueur, H. Peter, M.D., Head, Family Therapy Service, Waterbury State Hospital, Waterbury, Vt.

Napier, Augustus Y., Ph.D., Director of Training, Wisconsin Children's Treatment Center, and Clinical Instructor, Department of Psychiatry, University of Wisconsin, Madison, Wisc.

Pittman, Frank S. III, M.D., Director, Psychiatric Services, Grady Memorial Hospital, Atlanta, Ga.

Prosky, Phoebe, M.S.W., Staff and faculty member, Nathan W. Ackerman Family Institute, New York, N.Y.

Sander, Fred M., M.D., Director, Family Process Unit, Bronx Municipal Hospital Center, and Assistant Professor of Psychiatry, Albert Einstein College of Medicine, Bronx, N.Y.

Whitaker, Carl, M.D., Professor of Psychiatry, University of Wisconsin, Madison, Wisc.

Contents

Introduction

THIS *Seminars in Psychiatry* symposium has been assembled with the goal of providing the reader with an introductory overview of family systems psychotherapy with emphasis on clinical technique. The articles have been written mainly from a how-to-do-it point of view; the issue is subtitled a primer, "a small introductory book"..."a first means of instruction." As Sander notes in his bibliographical review in this issue, there is a proliferating literature in this field, six major collections of articles having appeared in book form in the last 2 yr alone. One adds yet another collection to this rising tide with caution. On the other hand, the expanding array of family therapy theories and techniques justifies an attempt at an introductory guidebook.

The number and variety of treatment methods in the mental health field has increased tremendously in the last two decades. Each major technical innovation reflects a somewhat differing view of the nature of human existence, of the reasonable goals of intervention, as well as of the most effective measures for accomplishing these goals. While it is possible to identify a number of salient dimensions along which mental health therapies may usefully be categorized, we are far from achieving any generally agreed-upon typology at this time. Thus, it is extraordinarily difficult to place family psychotherapy clearly in relationship to other modalities.

By most standards, the field is growing. At meetings of national organizations in the mental health field, each year finds larger proportions of the programs devoted to family therapy-related issues. The department of psychiatry of Georgetown University Medical School has been holding conferences on family therapy for a decade now; about 50 persons attended the first such conference and the number has risen each year until the most recent was attended by over 1000 persons. At a national conference on training in family therapy held this last year in Philadelphia, there were 900 persons in attendance. Subscriptions to the journal *Family Process* have risen approximately 15% a year and now stand at over 3000. The first family institute in America opened in New York in 1960; presently there are ten such family institutes in the U.S.

It is difficult to assess the meaning of this. Certainly there is a kind of faddish quality to it; it may represent a legitimate advance but also may reflect discouragement with other modes of psychotherapy because of poor training and psychologic resistances. To some degree, the issue is an economic and political one, as Bloch and LaPerriere note in this collection. Family therapy training has to some extent operated outside of traditional hierarchical professional structures.

This collection of articles may be read by the psychiatrically knowledgeable reader without any special training in the field of family systems psychotherapy, with a view to acquiring enough of a general sense of the field to begin some preliminary work in it. Training opportunities through workshops, teaching conferences, and through the organized teaching programs of the family institutes and departments of psychiatry are becoming increasingly more available. The field is new enough so that no final pattern of training has emerged. It is a reasonable guess that the inevitable process of bureaucratization will emerge, although the field has been self-consciously nonestablishmentarian up to this point.

The articles in this seminar are assembled for various reasons. The two introductory articles, by Bloch and LaPerriere, and Sander, are designed to provide a theoretical statement about the nature of family psychotherapy and an introduction to the spirit and substance of the literature in the field.

Next there is an article by Franklin and Prosky, which describes the issues and techniques of an initial family interview. Space and its relationship to family structure and therapy is then considered by the Duhls and Kantor, while two important tools of the family therapist, the clinical home visit and modern audio–visual equipment, are discussed by Bloch and Alger, respectively.

Family therapy has borrowed heavily from group therapy. Two articles describe the procedures for seeing families in groups. Laqueur, using a question and answer format, discusses the establishment of multiple family therapy groups, and Framo writes about his methods for working with a group of couples.

Pittman discusses the use of family therapy orientation and technique in managing acute psychiatric crises, and Napier and Whitaker complete this volume with a discussion of the problems of the beginning family therapist.

The reading lists that follow most of the articles are intended to be focused and highly selective additional reference materials; they are not intended to be comprehensive.

Family therapy is a burgeoning field, still in a rapid growth phase. Its final shape and content cannot as yet be clearly predicted.

Donald A. Bloch, M.D.

Techniques of Family Therapy:
A Conceptual Frame

Donald A. Bloch, M.D. and Kitty LaPerriere, Ph.D.

INTEREST in the family *of* the psychiatric patient has blended in recent years with an interest in the family *as* the psychiatric patient. This process began in child psychiatry, drew important technical skills from play therapy, group therapy, and psychodrama, with more recent additions from the encounter and training group fields. On the theoretical side, it has roots in anthropologic and sociologic studies of the family, in psychoanalytic theory, in the study of small groups, and, more recently, in linguistics, kinesics, general systems theory, and communications theory.

Family therapy is the face-to-face psychotherapy of a natural system, natural in contrast to a group formed specifically for the purpose of therapy. The therapist, or team of therapists, directly engages the family, or some substantial element of the family, of the index patient. Increasingly, families seek treatment without an identified patient for conditions defined in terms of the functioning of the entire family system, e.g., marital discord or generational conflict. What unites all family therapists is the view that change, which is significant to the psychotherapeutic endeavor, takes place in the family system. With this unifying thread, they may vary considerably as to the size of the elements of the family they engage, the techniques they employ, and the theory to which they adhere.

Historically, two parallel and comparatively unrelated movements comprise the family therapy field. One reflects the marriage counselling and child study traditions. The orientation to issues of the parent-child relationship and the marital relationship has been principally educational, built generally on the assumption that difficulties in these areas are the result of poor practices and can be dealt with by educational methods. Clinical family therapy grows out of the psychiatric and mental health movements; this article refers primarily to a body of knowledge originating from this latter area.

Several important changes in psychiatric theory and practice preceded the development of the family approach to psychiatric matters. In the decade following World War II, roughly from 1945–1955, a number of innovative themes were gathering force in American psychiatry. As the psychoanalytic movement consolidated its position, new approaches became theoretically influential. New definitions of the proper area of psychiatric concern as being the interpersonal field were developed, e.g., by K. Lewin and H.S. Sullivan. Interest in sociocultural factors were expressed in the work of K. Horney, C. Thompson, and F. Redlich. Psychiatric theory was also influenced by sociology and small group psychology,[26] communication theory,[31] and general systems theory.[14,35,40] Some-

Reprint requests should be addressed to Donald A. Bloch, M.D., Nathan W. Ackerman Family Institute, Inc., 149 E. 78 Street, New York, N.Y. 10021.

1

what later microkinesthesiologists undertook an exploration of the previously unnoticed areas of nonverbal communication.[6,33]

On the clinical side, there was growing attention in that decade to the effects of the social milieu on the patient, as seen in the studies relating hospital environments, individual psychologic performance, and treatment outcome.[8,36] Conceptions of the therapeutic community as a treatment modality were also having profound influence on developing concepts of psychotherapy.[20] Group therapy flourished as did psycho-drama. Of particular importance were the finely grained studies of the psychotherapy of schizophrenia,[12,38] which revealed a carefully articulated relationship between the bizarre, apparently incomprehensible symptomatology of the schizophrenic and the events taking place in the on-going interpersonal field.

Common to this welter of activity was consideration of the psychiatric patient and his treatment in terms of the *social systems* of which he was a part. In a sense, the process of abstracting the patient and his symptomatology from the background of interpersonal and social context–which had characterized the psychiatric and psychologic advances of the previous century—began to be reversed. Treatment came more and more to be conceptualized in terms of its relationship to the actual experiences—real time experiences—of the patient. An interactive rather than in-dwelling model of mental illness was increasingly favored, and an interactive model of psychotherapy came to dominate the thinking of a number of clinicians and theoreticians as well. A principle feature of this was the emphasis on the systems qualities of the phenomena being considered and of their conceptualizations in communications terms.

An interest in the family system as it related to psychiatric disorder inevitably evolved out of these trends. Clinically, there was a burgeoning effort to conceptualize psychiatric disorder in family terms and to initiate methods of family treatment on issues previously thought to express processes contained within the individual. The schizophrenias attracted considerable attention. A group in Palo Alto, Calif., led by Bateson, Jackson, Haley, and Weakland produced a series of landmark papers[5] elaborating the concept of family homeostasis and the double-bind theory of schizophrenogenesis.[41] Wynne and his co-workers at the National Institutes of Health produced an important series of studies relating cognitive style and family system boundary characteristics in families with schizophrenic members.[42] The Lidzes and Fleck at Yale[10] also investigated patterns of family interaction as these related to schizophrenia in an offspring. Their studies were cast somewhat more in psychoanalytic terms. They considered, for example, such matters as failure of the parent of the opposite sex to maintain properly the incest barrier as a pathogenic element in certain instances of schizophrenia, and they related this in turn to parental patterns of interaction and to certain parental character structures.

Depression and mourning were reconsidered in family terms, particularly the importance of concealed depression in influencing family interaction patterns.[27] Childhood phobias, as they related to unnoticed phobias and separation anxiety in parents, were elucidated by Ackerman[1] and others. Several investigators, including Ferreira and Jackson[17-19] studied somatization patterns in the family and began an evaluation of the relationship between family process and psychosomatic disease. Thus, from the early 1950s, there has been a steady expansion of family-oriented interest into all of the areas of clinical concern to psychiatry, in an attempt to understand psychiatric events as an expression of family process and, secondly, to develop techniques for intervention based on modification of interactive patterns of the entire family.

Concurrently, an embryo of research methodology and technology was developing. Wherever possible, the aim was to study processes characteristic of the entire family, a formidable undertaking considering its variability and complexity. One of the strategies has been to study the family as a small group, using techniques developed for study of other small group processes. The Bales interaction scales have been popular here.[2] A common procedure has been to present the family or some part of it with a standardized stressing task such as the Strodtbeck Revealed Differences Test[37] or the Ravich Interpersonal Game Test (RIG/T).[29] Many studies have addressed themselves to an analysis of the formal elements of speech as used by the family, Cheek, for example,[9] has dealt with characteristics of pronoun usage in families with schizophrenic members, while Haley[15] has attempted to build a mathematical model of speaker sequences and to define pathology in terms of deviation from randomness. Other workers have been interested in common projective patterns in families: Loveland,[23] for example, studied a Rorschach composed by the family, while Singer and Wynne[34] used projective tests to estimate family interaction potential. A recent review by Riskin and Faunce[30] may be consulted for a description of the current state of family interaction research.

ROOTS OF FAMILY PSYCHOTHERAPY

Family psychotherapy borrows many of its techniques from other fields. An important source has been *child psychiatry* when work with the child was extended into work with the child and mother. Later, fathers were added to the work so that a common treatment configuration had (and has) mother, father, and child with separate therapists. Alternatively, the child might work with the psychiatric therapist while mother and/or father have (lower status) consultations with the social worker. A logical outgrowth of these efforts was to conduct interviews with the entire family as a group, aiming to reduce the investment of therapeutic time, the hazards of family mis-communication and of concealed differences among therapists.

Child analysis was technically and conceptually invaluable; indeed, Freud's celebrated "Little Hans"[11] case was the first case both of child analysis and of family therapy, since the boy was treated through the agency of his father. As a single instance of the contribution of child analysis, we may note the relation of play therapy to family therapy. The earlier use of dolls and art materials to represent primary objects in play therapy with children led to a procedure in family therapy in which primary objects, i.e., mother, father, siblings, are used to represent themselves.

Group therapy in its diverse modes has made, and continues to make, technical contributions to family therapy. More recently concepts and methods of group therapy have been extended into the development of therapeutic formats in which couples (see Framo) and families (see Laqueur) are seen in groups.

Gestalt, transactional, and *encounter* styles or orientations (see Napier) have been picked up for use in the techniques of family therapy. *Games theory* and *communicational analysis* also have provided technical inputs, with some of their research procedures becoming a part of the therapeutic armamentarium, e.g., the Ravich interpersonal game test (RIG/T).

In the same way that primary objects in family therapy replace the dolls and toys of play therapy, so the actors of *psychodrama,* when used with families, are in part or wholly replaced by the original persons whose parts they play. In some cases, a mixture of family and nonfamily members is recruited to act out critical events in the family's life. Specific techniques of psychodrama have also been adapted for use in family psychotherapy; role playing, simulations, and "doubling" are among those that may be mentioned.

The field has had a steady orientation towards *direct* observation of the phenomena under consideration as opposed to dealing with *reports* about the phenomena. Thus, it has developed a teaching technology largely built around live supervision utilizing the one-way mirror and similar devices. An instance of this is the development of the clinical home visit as a diagnostic and treatment tool (see Bloch). In the same spirit, there is growing interest in the use of devices that can provide the family with additional vantage points for viewing their own behavior and patterns of interaction and the opportunity to study these in sequence and in detail. Modern television equipment (see Alger) is particularly useful in this regard and innovative hardware and software are flowering in this area.

SOME CHARACTERISTICS OF FAMILY THERAPY

Any attempt to distinquish family therapy as a technique must begin with a caveat. The field may not be more variegated within its confines than other psychotherapies, but it is certainly not less so. Thus, one generalizes at one's peril. No single set of descriptive terms quite captures the dry, acerbic, intellectuality of the theories and practices of Murray Bowen or the dramatic elan of Virginia Satir; we will not be able to do justice to these highly individual styles or those of other leaders in the field with our description. Yet, the characterization we attempt below is *mostly* correct. It should begin by recollecting the opening comment in this article to the effect that what unites family therapists is the intention to change the family system.

To characterize family therapy techniques then is, in large degree, to make distinctions of emphasis rather than of sharply defined differences. As noted earlier, the essence of family therapy as a technique is that it deals directly with a natural system, some substantial part of the family of the index patient (where an index patient has been defined). A series of technical and stylistic consequences flows from this: Thus, family therapy is an action therapy, a do-show-and-tell technique; a therapy of primary objects and first order symbols in which people are used to symbolize themselves; it is a therapy of confrontation; a therapy oriented towards direct exploration of systems feedback loops; a therapy oriented towards exchange of alternate vantage points, a therapy of actual exploration and trial of alternate modes of adaptive interaction. It is a modeling technique in which the therapist's use of self offers interpersonal modes for the family to copy.

It is not a therapy of abstinence in the hands of most practitioners, although Bowen[7] and his students are notable exceptions. Most often, it is an affective liberating technique. The family therapist may be actively involved in systems maintenance operations, such as nurturance, power balancing, and role and boundary definition.

The therapist is available as a whole person, actively using his own affective responses and, in a witting and deliberate way, the full range of his response patterns as measures and indicators of the nature of the events taking place.

> In the course of a family interview, a male therapist began to become aware of his own growing anger at the father of the family who seemed to be using deft, humorous, self-deprecating remarks to reduce awareness of painful feelings and so as not to notice pleas by other family members for support and love. The therapist in an irritated tone said that he did not like being "fobbed off" by the father. There followed an intense moment of silent eye-to-eye contact, after which the father said, "I don't want to fight with you." More silence followed and the father added, "either we would destroy each other or I would have to back down, and I prefer to back down." The therapist became aware that his own anger was replaced with a profound sense of sadness; tears welled in his eyes and he said to the father, "Would this be the only possible solution?". The two men continued looking at each other; not a sound was to be heard in the room. After a moment, the therapist became fully aware of the emotion that had been moving him and so said to the man, "I know what it feels like to be an isolated father." As he said this, tears began to stream down the father's face. Throughout, the family watched this display in silence.

The example illustrates a number of aspects of family therapy technique. The scene described was played out in the presence of the other family members; the index patient, an adult daughter, her older brother, and the mother. It was a confrontation of the father's defensive distancing; the confrontation was precipitated by direct action rather than by interpretation. An interpretation of the father's isolation was made by breaching it, rather than by referring to it. By allowing his own anger and sadness to be clearly visible and by using them as guides to the *meaning* of the events, the therapist modeled alternate modes for the father and the family.

From this point of view, the therapist is a person able to provide inputs that are vivid, flexible, and unexploitative. A family session is a safer place to do this than is the one-to-one dyadic interview. By its public nature, there is opportunity provided for experimentation with human interaction that might not be possible elsewhere.

Issues of the therapist's personal involvement (or lack of it) permeate all psychotherapies. In family therapy, they are somewhat more out in the open because the anonymity of the therapist is less taken for granted. In other therapies, personal interaction takes place against the barrier of noninvolvement; in family therapy, involvement is encouraged. Perhaps opening the door and inviting the devil in may be a safer procedure than pretending the door is closed and having the devil sneak in. While transferential expectations still exist, the format reduces the heated magical quality of dependent, erotic, and hostile fantasies for all family members. Jokes about sexual contact between therapist and patient, which are ubiquituous in psychoanalytic therapy, are practically unknown in family therapy.

Like all psychotherapies, family therapy clearly sets limits as to the nature of the real involvement, i.e. action, of the therapist with the patient family. He will make a clinical home visit but will not move in, be sexually appreciative but not have a sexual relationship, be angry but protective and facilitating. The symbolic nature of the psychotherapeutic encounter and the proscenium arch of therapy exists here as it does for all other psychotherapies, at least as far as the therapist is concerned. He is moved by the drama, but it is not his life.

Family therapy is explicitly concerned with the role of power in the therapeutic work. Power does not only develop transferentially, but also by interference with the system's options. Thus, the psychoanalyst principally is trying to divest himself of power; the flow of the work is first to increase then reduce his transferential power, to reverse the patient's infantile regressive sense of analytic omnipotence, and to reorient the relationship to equality and reality. The family therapist, aware of the highly stable nature of bio-psycho-social systems, is trying to grasp power. To this end, family therapy uses paradox, quirkiness, inconsistency, and reversals as deliberate systems disequilibrators. The promotion of disequilibration, *the anti-homeostatic theme of family therapy technique,* is a profound and important one. Many of the innovators in the field (J. Haley, C. Whitaker, M. Bowen) have been extraordinarily imaginative and inventive in developing such an armamentarium (see Napier).

As noted earlier, it is a modeling technique when the therapist demonstrates alternate moves by doing them *with* the family—by being *kind* to a frantically manipulative mother, *unafraid* of a tyrannical father, *supportive* of a pregnant 15-yr-old as she advises her parents about sex and love. Paradoxic and political elements, as well as modeling techniques, may be seen in all of these instances.

In this context, issues relating to qualities of the therapist as a person are prominent. It is important to note that the personal deficiencies of the therapist are often useful adjuncts to the therapeutic work; the inability of a therapist to deal with something is frequently as important as his ability to cope with it. He may be revealed as baffled or guarded, as responsive to the same pressures of social role, male power concerns, and nurturant needs and wishes, just as the members of the family may be. He can be inducted by the family into response patterns that mimic and in fact *reveal* the very difficulties and family itself is experiencing.

This version of counter-transference is different from what one sees in many individual psychotherapies. In addition, co-therapy teams may be used to display for the family an interaction that reflects splits, competitiveness, communication difficulties, role confusions, and so on. The subtle, textural elucidation of these interactional issues is extremely difficult in a dyad when one person, the psychotherapist, must be the screen on which these complexities are projected. Subtlety and richness are added when family members can use each other directly as well as the therapist(s) for these purposes.

Finally, it is a proselytizing therapy. The very orientation to family involved in this choice of format speaks for a value and belief system, which generally holds that a family or family-like system is, in fact, needed for the maintenance of mental health, that a human being functioning in isolation is underfunctioning or malfunctioning. In attempting to do justice to the basically social nature of human beings, to the fact that human life thrives only in intimacy, in taking into account the sociocultural system in which we all live, the assumption is that the family, despite its many drawbacks and uncertainties, is the most reliable and responsive system for maintaining the interpersonal connectedness of people.

INDICATIONS

Indications for family therapy may be categorized under two headings; occasions when it is *mandatory* and occasions when it is the *most desirable* approach. We will assume that family therapy means some kind of prolonged and regular contact with the family beyond an initial diagnostic-therapeutic assessment interview.

Family therapy is clearly the only suitable treatment in situations where the presenting problem appears in systems terms. This may involve conflict at one level of the system, e.g. a severe marital conflict or severe sibling rivalry, or it may involve intergenerational conflict and disturbance. Marital conflicts, sibling conflicts, and intergenerational conflicts are increasingly prevalent as presenting psychiatric complaints. These are essentially family systems complaints rather than complaints about individual psychologic difficulties. A traditional, individually oriented psychotherapist might suggest treatment for the most obviously disruptive, or most obviously suffering, person. Yet, one must suspect such efforts would abet the blame-laying and scapegoating operations of the family rather than promote the general improvement of patterns of communications, self-awareness, and affective interchange.

The direct threat to the integrity of the family system posed by the generational conflict or marital conflict makes a sufficiently clear statement as to the need for assistance interventions, so that no further justification is usually required of a therapist. Even here, an overly limited view of the size of the relevant family system may lead to a constricted therapeutic arrangement.

> The index patient was an eighteen-yr-old girl with an out-of-wedlock pregnancy. There was open and continued conflict between the parents and the girl over her behavior in general and in regard to plans for this pregnancy specifically. The parents wanted her to terminate the pregnancy with an abortion; her stated wish was to carry the child to term and place the baby for adoption. Much of the parental concern was centered around the issue of the reaction of the community to the pregnancy. While the generational conflict was the initial basis for the consultation, the first family interview revealed severe concealed disagreements between the parents, which were long-standing and antedate the present complaint, and seemed to be related to it, at least in the sense that the pregnancy restored and healed over a severe split between the girl's parents. Further study also demonstrated that the grandparental generation had opposed the parents' marriage and had been consistently involved in intense maneuvering designed to split the parental pair. The extended families of the girl's parents had never reconciled themselves to the marriage, nor had they been willing to free *their* children from bonds of dependency.

In the foregoing instance, it was necessary ultimately to involve elements of all three generations and of both extended families in order to explore and resolve the conflicts most efficiently. As the parents were able to clarify the nature of their own involvement with their own extended families and with *their* parents in particular, it was possible to reduce the intensity of their competitive struggle for their daughter's allegiance. This in turn permitted the girl to make an adequate decision about her pregnancy.

The more a clearly visible and close relationship exists between a subjectively experienced malfunction and its location in the interpersonal system, the more plausible is a systems intervention. This plausibility may, of course, be much greater for the therapist than for the family. Thus, the therapist's first task is to capture the family's interest in his view and to make the transition from subjective experience to systems experience. The success of the enterprise depends on the therapist's ability to locate and activate the connections that are frequently buried, frequently out of awareness, and relate them to the subjectively experienced dysfunction. It often comes as a surprise that grossly malfunctioning individual conditions are amenable to this translation into systems terms and become therapeutically accessible.

Symptomatic outbreaks associated with developmental transitions in the family are comparatively easy to conceptualize and demonstrate in these terms and often provide the tyro family therapist with good treatment cases. As the family moves through time, there are nodal developmental points in the flow of events. They are well known, are associated usually with a change in status for one or more family members, and are accompanied almost always by a reshuffling of functions, power relationships, and, therefore, almost always by stress.

A full recounting of these periods of transformation is inappropriate here, nor is it possible simply to relate symptomatic pictures to the stress source. Families are uniquely able to provide pooled information that will elucidate these issues, however; and there is no substitute for the conjoint family interview as a diagnostic tool in this regard. A general principle governing the degree to which they will be stressful concerns the reactivation of similar unresolved issues in the parental life.

Early childhood is critically important in that the infant's requirements for nurturance, dependent support, and protection are likely to intensify competition for such supplies when they are scarce in a family. This is, of course, particularly true when there are two infantile, immature, and undernurtured parents. Frequently, marital conflict will erupt in such families, usually around some symbolic representation of nurturance, such as money. At times, desperate efforts to solve the parenting needs of the young couple will lead to a rapid production of additional children, particularly in families from cultures that accord position and status to women and men with large numbers of children.

> The young mother of an Italian Catholic family came from stock close to its peasant origins in Calabria. Her first marriage was dissolved because of the infertility of her husband. She married a devout modern Italian-American Catholic businessman, whose first wife had died shortly after the birth of their only child. The marriage was consummated around the issue of child production and care, the husband being chosen for his demonstrated fertility, the wife because of her interest and apparent emotional availability for this purpose. The signal event in the courtship, from the husband's point of view, was the young woman's extravagant concern when she accidently burned his child with a cigarette, although this might also have forewarned him as to the ambivalence of her motives.
>
> With the birth of two children of her own, the mother became increasingly neglectful of the child of her husband's former marriage. The child eventually died of a condition that was unrelated to this neglect, whereupon the family began to experience the most severe stress, all of this leading in turn to separations alternating with three more pregnancies. At the time of referral, there were five children in the family under the age of seven, two walled-off,

isolated parents, living in separate worlds of home and business, with a further catastrophic breakdown threatening.

The most highly maladaptive solutions to human stress situations are always those which, in an effort to relieve the stress, in fact add to it. In systems terms, we would speak of this as error amplifying or positive feedback. The under-nurtured, poorly integrated parents in the above example consistently made the wrong moves by producing more children in an effort to solve the parenting problem. The referral for treatment was centered around the issue of marital incompatibility. The strategy of family treatment was to identify and reverse the pattern described above by initially providing large amounts of nurturant support for the parents.

Vulnerability to stress in the family is accentuated by the arrival of children in similar sex and sibling positions in relation to the new family as the parents were in relation to their families of origin. When this is coupled with a re-activation of relationship issues, as noted above, a more potent disequilibrator is brought into being.

> A family organized itself around issues of control and dominance. The mother defined herself as a "battler" in relationship to her cruel, dominating, tyrannical father. Her husband was chosen for his apparent docility. She was a first-born daughter. At the point where her oldest daughter became increasingly autonomous, around the age of two, severe stress began to appear in the marital relationship along with phobic symptoms in the wife.

The foregoing examples are given to illustrate the possibilities of systems interpretations related to the experience of stress associated with developmental change. This article cannot set the full range of these possibilities before the reader. His own imagination and life experiences will certainly provide much data for this viewpoint. One further example may be useful, coming as it does from the other end of life's continuum.

> A physician, the identified patient, an oncologist, experienced attacks of acute disabling anxiety at work. Two family systems appeared to be involved in this. This man, in his early forties, was often required to attend cancer patients with hopeless outcomes; his own father was severely senile and worsening at the time. During the same period, there had been a reduction in the usually close support given him by his wife, because she had reached the end of her childbearing years, and was reorienting herself to a status less tied to her home. The physician/husband's dependent push towards her was asynchronous with her moves toward autonomy, and she had been somewhat resentful of his increasing demands upon her.

In this last example, two developmental shifts act to disequilibrate a previously stable system. The move of the husband's father into severe senescence was associated with the wife's leaving the childbearing role and moving into a more separate and autonomous pattern of relatedness to the family. His work as a cancer specialist with the exposure to stresses associated with dying and mutilated patients set the stage for his symptomatic breakdown. (An associated factor is the failure to provide an adequate social support system for those in stressful occupations. The unspoken assumption is that the family will do so.) These stresses, however, had been reasonably well tolerated over the years, until the developmental shifts had taken place in both the family of origin and family of procreation.

The ideologic and epistemologic stance of the mental health clinician determines the format and scope of the inquiry and the nature of the concepts developed as to the therapeutic approach indicated. All of the examples given above could have been treated with other modalities. For example, the physician last described had been previously placed on large doses of chemotherapeutic agents.

Thus, the entire progression of life's stages is somewhat disequilibrating in the sense described above: The birth of successive children, particularly those in important sibling positions, the separation and departure of children for school, the achievement of sexual roles, identities and work statuses, middle age, and the developmental stages of later life. In this sense, of course, they are much like other intercurrent events: illness or death, financial reversal and good fortune. All can operate in this way to require adaptation on the part of the family system, or to activate latent conflictual areas.

As the relationship of the symptom or subjective disturbance to the systems property of the family is less clear, there is apparently also less warrant for family study and therapy, in the eyes of many observers. At this point it becomes quite literally an act of faith, at least for the neophyte family therapist, to ask the entire family to be part of the therapeutic work.

> A mother called to refer her 19-yr-old daughter for therapy for perineal pruritus of unexpected origin. Careful urologic work-up had revealed no genito-urinary pathology. The young woman was leaving the country in 3 mo. The symptom had existed for 5 yr, becoming increasingly incapacitating. At the therapist's request, the mother and father, her 28-yr-old sister and her 30-yr-old brother joined in an investigation of the family interaction. A treatment plan was developed which combined family meetings with individual psychotherapy by the same therapist. The essential configuration involved an extraordinarily tight tie between the mother and the index patient's older sister, who had had a severe, crippling illness at the age of 12. Associated with 4 yr of care, and intense close involvement subsequent to this, was a reversal in the patterns of parental relatedness. The middle child became the one closest to the parents. From that point on, the much-adored older brother and the index patient were moved to subsidiary positions. The index patient's decision to leave the country for schooling abroad was associated with an increase in her symptomatology, related to the rage and hurt over her inability to successfully fuse with her mother.

Subsequent to this therapeutic work, the patient's symptoms disappeared, she slept continuously through the night for the first time in years, and significant transformations in the family relatedness were achieved as well. As noted, the choice of family and individual therapy could not be dictated by any a priori understanding of the relationships between the presenting complaint and the systems properties of the family. That could only be done post hoc, and the suggestion that the consultation be arranged as it was was entirely on the basis of the clinician's preference as to the most economical and effective way for dealing with sociopsychologic problems.

Increasing awareness of the collusion of marital partners in situations that present as addictive (e.g., alcohol, drugs) or as primary sexual difficulties (impotence, premature ejaculation, frigidity) has led to an awareness of the importance of uncovering the stake the so-called well partner has in the illness of the identified patient. The treatment of choice is either couples or family therapy. Frequently, this is associated with behavior modification therapy, but the requirement is still for both the marital partners to participate in the work.

Many psychotherapists have their first experience with family therapy in the course of investigating a therapeutic impasse that has occurred in their practices. The patient has failed to thrive, and the data begin to suggest collusive involvement in the pathology by either a mate or other family members. The individual awareness of this does not seem to develop enough potency to fully break through the circular patterns, and the therapist seeks consultation with a colleague who has a family orientation.

Thus, for the family therapist, family therapy is the treatment of choice in all conditions where psychotherapy is indicated, unless some contraindications to its use can be established.

CONTRAINDICATIONS

There are obviously many conditions of human existence that are not treated with psychotherapy of any kind. One might think of situations associated more with economic and political issues, with broad social issues, or, at the other extreme, with biologic issues. In considering indications and contraindications of family therapy, the comparison is principally with individual psychotherapy, with the use of drugs and with such measures as hospitalization.

A pragmatic base underlies the decision not to do family therapy. Psychiatric nosology is no more a guide to treatment suitability here than elsewhere in psychiatry; there are no diagnostic conditions per se that are not treatable by this modality. Two things determine unsuitability. One is the *capability of the individual family therapist,* that is, his ability to engage families and hold them in treatment. Second, there is the *willingness of the family system* to experience the difficulties attendant upon change. To give up scapegoating of an identified patient may simply require experiencing intolerable discomfort so that treatment breaks up, or the family breaks up.

As noted earlier, family psychotherapy is considered to be among the safer interventions. Malignant paranoid conditions, particularly where there is a history of open violence, are considered to be best avoided and to lend themselves more to individual psychotherapeutic efforts. Family psychotherapy has, in one of our cases, precipitated two paranoid schizophrenic episodes in a marriage of stabilized social isolates.

> The wife was the index patient in this instance. She had adapted to a childless, lonely, restricted married life, spending most of her time cleaning and caring for a tiny, immaculate apartment, while her highly successful executive husband occupied himself with 16-hr work days at his factory. This functioning adaptation was twice upset by efforts of the childless couple to become more intimate with each other, under the guidance of a family therapist. Each effort seemed brilliantly successful, with heightened sexual contact and enjoyment and an increase in shared activities, but each instance led to a psychotic decompensation for the wife, under the unmanageable pressures of this increased intimacy.

Pittman, in an article entitled "Treating the Doll's House Marriage,"[28] has described another limitation of family psychotherapy in which a relationship between a dependent partner and a protective, manipulative, managerial mate is disequilibrated by the efforts of a therapist or other growth-enhancing third person, with poor result. The manageable adaptation, which protected both partners, is fractured but not replaced. In these instances it is the author's phrase: "Better to leave bad enough alone."

While family psychotherapy is the treatment choice in most child psychiatric problems, at the very least as part of the study process, there are contraindications as well if the child's physical or emotional health is at such great risk that the advantages of working with him in the natural family setting are offset by the dangers. Residential treatment institutions have found it helpful to devote considerable therapeutic effort to direct work with the families of the children they serve, even while the child is out of the home, so that he will not be returned to a pathogenic situation.

On occasion, family psychotherapy is contraindicated, not because of the dangers of catastrophic breakdown, but rather because of the extremely poor prognosis for change in the family group. Thus, there are "dead" families or nonfamilies, meaning by these terms aggregates of individuals living in some role structure like a family, e.g., father, mother, and children, but where lack of affective vitality permeates the fabric of relatedness to the point where there is a permanent and apparently irreversible elimination of emotionally meaningful interchanges. Most commonly, there is unremitting defensiveness, affective flattening and unresponsiveness, coupled with a total lack of confrontation and challenge. Repeatedly, issues are dealt with by denial, obfuscation, and affective inappropriateness. These families can be distinguished from depressed families, who seem to show a reduction in vitality but permit the joint experience of pain and depressive effect. They are often families in which one member is schizophrenic. As Shaffer et al.[32] have noted, the difficulty of treating them appears to be related to the capacity of the family to induct the treating person into their own affective-cognitive system by successfully attacking the therapist's sense of continuity and relatedness.

Modifications of technique often seem to be necessary with such families, perhaps partly to protect the therapist's sanity. Some of the more promising variants on this have been multiple family therapy (see Laqueur) and multiple impact therapy.[25] In both instances, the direct effect on the therapists is diluted by concentrations of auxiliary personnel or by working with more than one family at the same time.

At times, the judgment may be that to disturb long-standing equilibria in a family may produce a catastrophe. If we assume that distance operations, unrelatedness, and isolation in the family are maintained as security measures, bringing the family together for therapy may shift these defensive operations so as to free unmanageable affect, with the consequence that the family would mercilessly attack and destroy one of its members, or the therapist, or the functioning integrity of the family system.

In such instances, the endeavor to engage them is going to fail. Might it not best be omitted from the beginning? In some situations, one family member, usually the designated patient, insists or hopes that his family system can change. Even when this seems unlikely, the very fact of attempting the engagement, with the patient's knowledge, says something to the patient about what his reality is, and helps him move from an unreal expectation toward his family, which might be hopelessly and inappropriately maintained, toward a more suitable position of resignation. It may be important, for example, to bring into therapy aged parents who may well be beyond the point of involvement or change so as to finally put to rest their middle-aged offspring's expectations that magic and bounty and power will flow from those close to death. Equally, in a marital situation, where one partner is markedly more alive, growth oriented, or related than the other, it may be necessary to bring this into awareness so that realistic expectations can be formulated and options made explicit rather than kept blurred and hidden.

In some of these situations, however, basic value issues come into play. For instance, when do you leave well enough, or bad enough, alone? When is it better not to touch a family limping along in a walled-off, unrelated way, with a sense of great dissatisfaction on everybody's part, if the option is to uncover the discrepancies, to uncover the pain, and have the family members fly apart as isolated individuals with no viable alternatives of relatedness?

The issue cannot be satisfactorily resolved on a priori grounds. The experienced therapist makes great efforts in such instances to let the family tell him what its range of choices is and what choice is preferred.

PHENOMENOLOGY OF FAMILY THERAPY

Basically, the phenomenon of family therapy for any therapist consists of his engagement, with or without a co-therapist, of some social unit called the family in a therapeutic venture. He may have observed simulated interviews, seen video tapes, watched motion pictures, read articles and books, listened to lectures. He may be a solo practitioner distant from large teaching centers, or a mental health trainee at an institute or in a university department. He may be at one or another developmental stage in regard to his family of origin and in regard to his family of procreation. Whatever the nature of these prior events and circumstances may be, there is a final engagement with the family in the therapeutic venture, and the systems properties and informational properties of this engagement generate the phenomena of family therapy.

A high degree of dissonance-avoiding complementarity is a distinctive feature of communication in all natural systems. Since the family system has the longest tenure for individuals and is operative at earliest ages and during the years of highest new learning rates, the mutual integration of such patterns takes place most effectively among family members. One important feature of the phenomenology of family therapy concerns the large quantities of data that must be processed by the family therapist. Initially, the experience of shifting from a dyadic form of therapy to an interview session involving a family group is overwhelming. The data are more numerous by far, the interaction rate is high; of particular importance is the fact that a natural social group is producing the information, very often idiosyncratically, coded with considerable condensation and with high specificity of messages.

Thus, the sense of bewilderment and of information overload, which characterizes the therapist in a family treatment situation, is understandable. Theory building and the development of a set of basic treatment maneuvers and regularities help the therapist to stay afloat in a sea of data. Second, and more important, is an altered relationship with his own inner experience. This might be generally described as a shift from slower, controlled, cognitive examination of data towards more rapid affective processing. Minimal internal bodily and

affective clues within the therapist become more significant factors in the therapeutic process.

Because of the special information processing characteristics, the theory
building requirements and the active intervention that are required of him by
his engagement with the material, the family therapist is less able to isolate and
exclude the experience by excessive professionalism.

Related also is the increased importance of context as it bears on the experience, context referring to the physical and social circumstances in which the
therapist works, and the sociocultural circumstances under which the family
lives. After all, family *is* context.

The family therapist becomes increasingly aware of the effect on the nature of
the encounter of the social circumstance of *his* personal and professional life.
These determine the nature of the possible contractual relationships that can be
established. With the family defined as the patient, his philosophy of health and
illness is tested, and alternate models of illness must be considered, leading
frequently to conflicts with the other social fields in which he operates. The
terms "reality" and "pathology" may diminish their applicability as useful
concepts to those involved in this kind of engagement. Associated with that is
an altered distinction of the nature of the barrier between work and personal
life. This leads to the most important of these conflicts, the impact of family
therapy on the life of the therapist and his own family, as these are forced into
an altered state of relationship with the events of his new professional experiences.

Faced with this experience, the family therapist first of all has to revise some
of his concepts of individual psychopathology. He is led into issues of family
dynamics, into concepts related to systems rather than to individuals; he begins
to think in terms of family functions, family tasks, family developmental issues,
family interfaces with other systems, rather than in terms of success or failure
of the coping mechanism of one individual; he thinks in terms of the historical
multi-generational family; he thinks in terms of maintenance and restoration of
function rather than in terms of cure. Theory building becomes increasingly
important. At this point, there are several theoretical emphases, none of which
is comprehensive and rigorous, or sufficiently defined as to be predictive in a
statistically reliable way. However, the theories are sufficiently formulated to
inform the clinician how he is to proceed further and to make him look at the
families he works with in a particular way. Most useful are those approaches
conceptualized in general systems terms, an approach that increasingly has
come to dominate family therapy theorizing.

SYSTEMS ISSUES

This article will not attempt at any length to set out the principles of a general
systems approach to human behavior. The interested reader may consult
Grinker,[14] Gray and Duhl,[13] and von Bertalanffy.[40] Certain orienting points,
however, are of value in conceptualizing the relationship of the family systems
approach to other modes of intervention.

The first issue has to do with the ordering of phenomena at various levels
of complexity, that is, that there is a hierarchy of organization, each level of

which subsumes the levels underneath it. For our purposes, we can speak of a biochemical level of organization, an intrapersonal level, an interpersonal level, and a sociocultural level. In general, it would be assumed that the phenomena can be discovered to have representations at all of these levels.

As an example, we might consider depression in a woman. To schematize, the *biochemical level* might be represented by the correlation of her depression with hormonal changes during the menstrual cycle; the *intrapersonal level* by the use of depression as a mode of managing hostile affect; the *interpersonal level* by the coercive use of the depressive position, expressed in family terms by the function of her depressed position in the maintenance of overall patterns of family adaption; and the *sociocultural level* by the preferred modes of acculturation of females in a society that requires damming up assertive impulses.

In this sense, one would not make a distinction between any of these levels as being more *real,* although in any particular instance an intervention aimed to produce change in the behavior might strategically or tactically choose a particular level as being (1) more responsive to intervention and/or (2) more etiologically concerned with the phenomenon at hand.

The family approach to psychotherapy assumes that human behaviors ordinarily of concern to the psychiatrist and psychotherapist are behavioral expressions on the individual level of patterns of family systems functioning, and that they are most economically or affectively amenable to being modified by intervention at the family systems level. It is important to recognize that these are two different criteria for the choice of level of intervention. Thus, for example, one might very well regard a depression as being psychogenic in origin, but choose to treat it biochemically.

The systems issue comes up in terms of the size and membership of the unit held to be psychiatrically relevant. Family therapists are uniquely oriented towards a structure that goes beyond the parent-child relationship. It extends over three and four generations and includes, at a minimum, the families of origin of both parents of the procreative family.

This interest in the generational structure involves such matters as family myths, secrets, identity positions, as well as the transmission of central thematic aspects of family adaptive strengths, stress vulnerability, and principle defensive operations. This is not to ignore that the organizing properties of personality provide important parameters of these phenomena: The individual acts on his environment and creates a kind of "portable reality." He selectively perceives elements in the social field that are critical to the maintenance of his security systems, and manages not to notice events that would be disruptive. A systems-oriented approach to these issues notes the repetitive, or replicative, patterns of social interactions and responses as they maintain the initial adaptive patterns developed in the early years of the child's life. The essential issue here is that one gives greater emphasis to *external feedback loops,* as they are critical to the maintenance of personality patterns, as opposed to the internal organization of psychic structures. This leads to family therapy as the logical intervention, which needs to occur in the current social system, since it is the response patterns brought into being there that are most effective in preventing change in the target behaviors.

Perhaps the most important systems concept as far as family therapy is concerned is that of homeostasis. It refers to the tendency of a system to maintain a dynamic equilibrium around some central tendency, and to undertake operations designed to restore that equilibrium when it is threatened in some way. Homeostasis has been a useful concept to the clinician in that it orients him to a mode of inquiry that asks of new behavior how it is adaptive to disequilibration and how it acts to restore prior integrative patterns.

The choice of intervention at the family level, then, is based on the double conception that the etiologic issue is being faced, and that, the importance of the maintenance of target behaviors by current life experience is being dealt with by strategically potent intervention aimed at interrupting circular patterns. In this sense, other psychotherapies are derivative, in that they hope, by producing changes in the patient's psychic organization, to lead him in turn to produce other modes of response in those with whom he principally interacts. The expectation is that by this process the social systems of which he is a part ultimately can be induced to change their patterns of response to him. The problem is that social systems like other psycho–biologic systems are metastable. Thus, all persons involved are engaged in stability maintenance, i.e., homeostasis, similar to the index patient. The logic of this makes change difficult unless it is at the level of the critical system involved.

In family terms, we are speaking about the maintenance of a dynamic equilibrium. Variation in human behavior becomes understandably functional; shifts in one part of the family system are disequilibrating and induce shifts elsewhere in the system. By knowing about this and taking advantage of it, family therapy aims to be effective.

POLITICAL ISSUES

It is good to know that political consequences flow from the assumption of a family therapy stance. We speak of politics here as those behaviors concerned with the acquisition and maintenance of power or those that exert influence on shifts in the power balance.

The recognition of the power orientation of supposedly nonpolitical social units, such as the mental health apparatus, or the family, is often experienced as distressing, indeed cynical, and frequently unworthy, yet the failure to do so is seriously handicapping. In regard to the family, such recognition must move in three directions: (1) to an understanding of the internal politics of the family;[21] (2) to an awareness of the political nature of the therapeutic encounter with the family (the therapist's interest in acquiring power); and, (3) to knowledge of the political effects in the mental health institutional world of a shift from individual orientations to a family orientation.

The process of identifying a psychiatric matter in family terms is, among other things, a political act. It shifts the power relations within the family, for example, by improving the status of the identified patient or by redirecting control operations away from a scapegoat. In addition, as we have noted, the family therapist is concerned with the acquisition of power in the family and uses many of his techniques explicitly for this purpose. He interferes directly in the family political system, making covert operations explicit and, on occasion, shifting his weight in the direction of redistributions of power of various sorts.

It is important to note, too, that the politics of family therapy, as of other mental health postures, extends into other arenas, most particularly the mental health apparatus. The institutions affected by and having an influence on this to the greatest extent are those directly concerned with the provision of services, clinics, child care agencies, family agencies, residential treatment facilities, hospitals, and the private practice apparatus.

These are some of the general consequences of this shift. Briefly, family therapy blends into work modes and technologies habitually associated with lower status elements of the mental health profession. Psychologists, social workers, nurses, para-professionals, and guidance personnel all participate in such work to the degree that they are competent. There are no clearly defined exclusive tools or techniques. The guarding of guild-like vocational interests is less possible under such circumstances unless a vast and rigid certification program were to be undertaken as in psychoanalysis. The temper of the times and the character of the work both seem to preclude this.

To this extent, that the personality and self of the therapist are a critical part of the therapeutic instrument, it is an instrument widely distributed among humans. To the extent that the medical model of a diseased person is deliberately eschewed, it is hard to claim the authority of special expertness. The spread of this modality is facilitated by other pressures in the modern world: the need to reduce the cost of services, to increase their availability, to provide access for nonacademic persons to suitable career lines. The net effect of this is to produce a lateralization of power and to reduce the power of the traditionally organized vertical hierarchies of psychiatry, psychology, and nursing in the mental health apparatus. In a variety of ways, established institutions have had to deal with these political issues, and the manner in which this has been done has, in turn, impinged on the degree of acceptance of family therapy. Thus, the choice of this approach for any practitioner becomes, in part, a political as well as a clinical act.

Finally, we may also speak of the moral and value position of family therapy. For a variety of reasons, the family is no longer easily recognizable as an institution organized around a task function or structure. More and more we expect to find our innermost needs for recognition, expression, validation, and intimacy satisfied within some family-like structure, or perhaps, mostly as adults, within the marriage relationship. Communication, openness, vulnerability, and genuineness become highly prized under these circumstances, in contrast to such values as adaptation, stability, safety, and permanence. In this sense, family therapy may be a statement for authenticity, for confrontation, for affective expression, for open conflict rather than a statement for an unchanging maintenance of a structure, a clearly defined fulfillment of a task, and a clearly expected social function. Said in another way, the interface between family and society is more permeable and less clearly defined, the expectations and inputs are many, and, consequently, a family represents a meeting place of many cultural subsystems negotiated via their individual representatives. No therapist will claim that he works to save families; rather he treats people in the context of family. Nevertheless, there is an underlying bias in favor of some such ongoing interrelatedness with consequential emphasis on the therapeutic choices to be made.

REFERENCES

1. Ackerman NW: Psychodynamics of Family Life, Diagnosis and Treatment in Family Relationships. New York, Basic Books, 1958

2. Bales RF: Interaction Process Analysis. Reading, Mass, Addison-Wesley, 1950

3. Bateson G: The biosocial integration of behavior in the schizophrenic family, in Ackerman NW, Beatman FL, Sherman S (eds): Exploring the Base for Family Therapy. New York, Family Service Association of America, 1961

4. Bateson G: Minimal requirements for a theory of schizophrenia. Arch Gen Psychiatry 2:477–491, 1960

5. Bateson G, Jackson DD, Haley J, Weakland J: Toward a theory of schizophrenia. Behav Sci 1:251–264, 1956

6. Birdwhistell RL: An approach to communication. Fam Process 1:194–201, 1962

7. Bowen M: A family concept of schizophrenia, in Jackson DD (ed): The Etiology of Schizophrenia. New York, Basic Books, 1960

8. Caudill WA: The Psychiatric Hospital as a Small Community. Cambridge, Mass, Harvard Univ Pr, 1958

' 9. Check F: Family interaction patterns and convalescent adjustment of the schizophrenic. Arch Gen Psychiatry 13:138–147, 1965

10. Fleck S, Lidz T, Cornelison A: Comparison of parent-child relationships of male and female schizophrenic patients. Arch Gen Psychiatry 8:1–7, 1963

11. Freud, S: Analysis of a phobia in a five-year-old boy, in Collected Papers vol. 3. London, Hogarth Press, 1949, pp. 149–289

12. Fromm-Reichman I: Principles of Intensive Psychotherapy. Chicago, University of Chicago Press, 1950

13. Gray, W, Duhl, FJ, Rizzo, ND (eds): General Systems Theory and Psychiatry. Boston, Little, Brown, 1969

14. Grinker R, (ed). Toward a Unified Theory of Human Behavior. New York, Basic Books, 1956

15. Haley J: Speech sequences of normal and abnormal families with two children present. Fam Process 6:81–97, 1967

16. Haley J: Whither family therapy? Fam Process 1:69–100, 1962

17. Jackson DD (ed): The study of the family. Fam Process 4:1–20, 1965

18. Jackson DD (ed): The question of family homeostasis. Psychiatr Q (Suppl) 31:79, Part 1, 1957

19. Jackson DD, Yalom I: Family research on the problem of ulcerative colitis. Arch Gen Psychiatry 15:410–418, 1966

20. Jones M: The Therapeutic Community. New York, Basic Books, 1953

21. Laing RD: The Politics of the Family. Toronto, CBC Publications, 1969

22. Laqueur HP, La Burt HA, Morong E: Multiple family therapy, in Wasserman JH (ed): Current Psychiatric Therapies, vol. 4. New York, Grune & Stratton, 150–154, 1964

23. Loveland NT, Wynne LC, Singer, MF: The family rorschach: a new method for studying family interaction. Fam Process 2:187–215, 1963

24. Lidz R, Lidz T: Homosexual tendencies in mothers of schizophrenic women. J Nerv Ment Dis 149:229–235, 1969

25. MacGregor R, et al: Multiple Impact Therapy with Families. New York, McGraw-Hill, 1964

26. Parsons T, Bales RF, Family Socialization and Interaction Process. Glencoe, Ill, Free Press, 1955

27. Paul NL: The role of mourning and empathy in conjoint marital therapy, in Zuk GH, Boszormenyi-Nagy I (eds): Family Therapy and Disturbed Families. Palo Alto, Calif, Science and Behavior Books, 1967

28. Pittman, F: Treating the doll's house marriage. Fam Process 9:143, 1970

29. Ravich RA: A system of notation of dyadic interaction. Fam Process 9:297–300, 1970

30. Riskin and Fauce: Fam Process 11, 1972

31. Ruesch J, Bateson G: Communication, the Social Matrix of Psychiatry. New York, Norton, 1951

32. Schaffer L, Wynne LC, Day J, et al: On the nature and sources of the psychiatric experience with the family of the schizophrenic. Psychiatry 25:32–45, 1962

33. Sheflen AE: Stream and Structure of Communicational Behavior. Philadelphia, Eastern Pennsylvania Psychiatric Institute, Behavioral Studies Monograph I, 1965

34. Singer MT, Wynne LD: Differentiating characteristics of parents of childhood schizophrenics, childhood neurotics, and young adult schizophrenics. Am J Psychiatry 120:234–243, 1963

35. Spiegel JP: A model for relationships among systems, in Grinker RR (ed): Toward a Unified Theory of Human Behavior. New York, Basic Books, 1956

36. Stanton R, Schwartz M: The Mental Hospital. New York, Basic Books, 1954

37. Strodtbeck FL: Husband-wife interaction over revealed differences. Am Sociol Rev 16: 468–473, 1951

38. Sullivan HS: The Interpersonal Theory of Psychiatry. New York, Norton, 1953

39. Thompson C: Interpersonal Psychoanalysis. New York, Basic Books, 1964

40. von Bertalanffy L: General System Theory. New York, Braziller, 1968

41. Watzlawick P: A review of the double bind theory. Fam Process 2:132–153, 1963

42. Wynne LC, Ryckoff I, Day J, et al: Pseudo-mutualization in the family relations of schizophrenics, in Bell NW, Vogel EF (eds): A Modern Introduction to the Family. Glencoe, Ill; Free Press, 1960

Touring the Literature of Family Therapy

Fred M. Sander, M.D.

CONTEXT OF FAMILY THERAPY

*Where family and nation once stood, or Church and
Party, there will be hospital and theatre too.[1]*

AT historical moments of cultural change such as ours, it is with considerable anxiety that we witness our most stable institutions and deeply held
convictions being called into question. Our parents are increasingly unable to
transmit their culturally acquired wisdom to us; we as parents, in turn, sense
our emerging obsolescence to our children. These doubts reflect more than the
ubiquitous and perennial waves of generational conflict. There is, rather, a tide
of cultural upheaval that defies our control and full understanding. We are too
profoundly enmeshed in the swirl of events to view them clearly or dispassion-
ately, and yet certain trends are becoming evident.

As Weston LaBarre has so convincingly documented in *The Ghost Dance,*[37] it
is at times of "cultural crises" that charismatic cult leaders emerge, satisfying
regressive needs, and that pseudo-religious movements begin. Henry Ellenberger has shown how this phenomenon is also true of the emergence of schools of
psychotherapy, beginning, for example, with Mesmer in pre-Revolutionary
France.[21] Where traditional religions have lost their sense of legitimacy, therapeutic institutions and varied "healers" have assumed a larger role in inte-
grating man in his social order. Philip Rieff has called our age, and aptly has
titled his recent book, *Triumph of the Therapeutic.* As another "professional
mourner at the wake of Christian culture," Rieff views with some apprehension
the emergence of psychologic man, who has gained a "self" while lacking some
compelling self-integrating communal purpose. He expects that "modern society will mount psychodramas far more frequently than its ancestors mounted
miracle plays, with the patient–analysts acting out their inner lives."[49]

No institution has been more altered by the rapidity of social change than
that transmitter of culture and that crucible of personality formation, the
family. I have elsewhere discussed this as a primary factor in the emergence of
the family therapy movement.[51] This movement has both the characteristics of a
revivalistic "Ghost Dance" and those of a new paradigm within the behavioral
sciences. As the lens of the psychotherapeutic looking glass is changed, new
structures are being seen and described. As mental illnesses are viewed increasingly as symptoms of family dysfunction, new patterns of family interaction are being described. It is in this sense that Szasz's *The Myth of Mental
Illness*[58] can be seen better in historical perspective. He was one of the first
to recognize the need for a paradigmatic change in the medical model of mental

*Reprint requests should be addressed to Fred M. Sander, M.D., Family Process Unit, Bronx
Municipal Hospital Center, Albert Einstein College of Medicine, 1300 Morris Park Avenue, Bronx,
N.Y. 10461.*

illness. By insisting that mental illnesses were more correctly viewed as "problems in living," he highlighted the limitations of that model. Inasmuch as
these "problems in living" are partly interactional difficulties, the family and
other immediate reference groups of an "identified patient" come into focus. By
insisting, however, on the absolute separation of brain disease from "problems
in living," Szasz's writings have, among other things, further polarized the
nature–nurture controversy in psychology.[52]

This new attention to interpersonal patterns in natural groups is producing a
vastly expanding literature. In this literature are reflected the multiple and
varied approaches, philosophies, prejudices, and orientations of the many
disciplines that have turned to the family as the unit of study. In 1971, Glick
and Haley[26] published a bibliography of writings in the field. Since the publication 2 yr ago[53] of our didactic course at the Albert Einstein College of
Medicine, six anthologies related to family therapy alone have been published.[2,22,30,31,50,57] This primer adds yet another volume to this expanding literature.

In this article, I shall outline *the overview of our literature course for family
therapy trainees,* rather than attempt the presently impossible task of a comprehensive review of the literature. The last three sections of the paper are
drawn from the earlier description of our course.[53]

The underlying goals which we attempt to achieve with this course are:
(1) Some historical perspective on the family as an institution; (2) awareness of
the multiple theoretical approaches to the understanding of family process;
(3) an appreciation of the difficulties in the scientific study of family forces in
the complex etiology of psychopathology; and (4) a comparison of writings of
various family therapists with videotapes or films of their work.

HISTORICAL PERSPECTIVE AS SEEN IN FICTION

During the course of a year-long, weekly, $1\frac{1}{2}$-hr seminar, we spend three to
four sessions on works of fiction that reflect changes in the structure and
function of "the family" and its sociocultural contexts from biblical times to
the present. The following capsule analyses illustrate our approach to the use
of such materials. The reader interested in such a literary review might organize
a study group of interested persons utilizing these or comparable readings.

The Book of Genesis (Abraham and Sarah)

Be fruitful and multiply and replenish the earth, and subdue it.[11]

To survive in the desert, nomads required a cohesive and authoritarian
family. The survival of the family clan of 50–200 tent-dwelling shepherds demanded obedience to the father. Individual survival was linked directly to
immediate and proximate membership in the family. To be out of this family
group was tantamount to death. The constant dangers of hostile tribes, animals,
and disease made regular claims on their numbers and gave birth to a moral
demand system whose first commandment was to be "fruitful and multiply."

This cultural demand system led barren Sarah to entrust Hagar, her hand-
maiden, to Abraham for the purpose of bearing his child. The inevitable
jealousies between Hagar and Sarah after the birth of Ishmael were followed

by the arbitrary banishment of Hagar and Ishmael. This banishment and the later test of Abraham's faith in the sacrificing of Isaac illustrate the unquestioned acceptance of the requirements of obedience to the father (and God the Father) in this evolving patriarchal culture.

The role of arranged marriages is illustrated in the marriage of cousins Isaac and Rebecca. The incest taboo, endogamy requirements, and reduction of intertribal hostilities all were served by such arrangements.

Isaac, the younger of Abraham's sons, inherited the family line following the exile of Ishmael. This began a pattern, repeated in subsequent generations, of the preference of the younger son over the older. In reviewing this literature, our study group speculated about the possible mechanisms for the generational transmission of such family patterns, while noting also how this theme of the "chosen son" resonated with the Jews' cultural self-representation as the "chosen people." Psychology, sociology, and culture were seen here as interwoven threads in the tapestry of Jewish history.

Jane Austen's Pride and Prejudice (Elizabeth and Darcy)

> It is a truth universally acknowledged, that a single man in
> possession of a good fortune must be in want of a wife.[1]

Marital arrangements in 18th-century English aristocracy served to sustain and support a complex structure of property in the form of entitlements. The above prophetic opening sentence of the novel reflects the demand system of that particular culture in the same sense that "to be fruitful and multiply" was part of the cultural demand system of the ancient Hebrews.

From the beginning, Elizabeth and Darcy capture our interest because they represent some transcendance over the rigidified and mannered demands of their culture. The commands of the covenant in the Old Testament are replaced here by the pressures of social forms, but there is some room for autonomy. Jane Austen weaves their strivings for greater independence of their backgrounds with their ultimate reconciliation with it. Their marriage, based on love rather than on propertied arrangements, ultimately supports and sustains the social order at the same time that it satisfies their quest for individual autonomy. Family requirements and individual strivings here are balanced at this threshold of the industrial revolution. Elizabeth is also clearly a forme fruste of the "emancipated modern woman."

T.S. Eliot's The Cocktail Party[20] (Edward and Lavinia) and Edward Albee's Who's Afraid of Virginia Woolf?[4] (George and Martha)

Where the Old Testament's first commandment to be fruitful and multiply served to facilitate the survival of a people, we are for the first time in the history of our civilization aware that our future hinges on our ability to contradict that precept. Both of these contemporary plays are of interest in this regard because they portray childless marriages. The Cocktail Party dramatizes a "modern couple" devoid of extended kinship. Living in an urban apartment, they find that their relationship is stabilized by infidelities and ultimately by the ministrations of the first family therapist in literature. This play, written in 1949, interestingly preceded the emergence of the family therapy movement in the 1950s and illustrates the socioreligious role of the psychiatrist in the secular society.[51]

In Albee's play, George and Martha battle endlessly as they desperately attempt to form a new family of friends and colleagues in a small college community. They do not sustain and support any viable culture, nor does any culture sustain and support them. They act out a "family romance" fantasy in which life is made bearable through the creation of an imaginary child.[12]

The historical perspective afforded by these readings in fiction highlights the emergence of the "modern nuclear family" as a unique structure in many ways while still containing certain universal attributes dictated by the biologic trimorphism of mother, father, and developing child. These ideas can be studied further in the readings of various other disciplines in which theories regarding the institution of the family are offered.

THEORIES OF THE FAMILY

As psychiatry has little to offer yet in the way of a comprehensive theory of families, a brief survey of the theories and descriptions of other disciplines affords the student some beginning orientation to the family.

In our readings, we considered the family as a social entity, its history and structure, rather than the individual family member, his biology and psychology. Beginning with Aries' *Centuries of Childhood*[6] the student can view the historical development of the idea of "the family," and the rather recent appearance of such values as intimacy, privacy, and the specialness of children. One can contrast the cultural anthropology of Levi-Strauss[39] and Margaret Mead[41] with the primatological writings of Jane van Lawick Goodall[27] for two different views of the family's universality. One can then examine the extent to which some of its institutions, such as sex role differences, childbearing, and incest-taboo, are biologically or socially obligatory. Readings in Parsons[43,44] show how one sociologic theory attempted to integrate biology, psychoanalytic psychology, sociology, and anthropology. This ambitious and little-appreciated effort is clearly a neglected precursor of what is referred to today as general systems theory. Communication and system theorists such as Haley[28-30] and Jackson[32-35,60] construct a family theory that dispenses with almost all the values, assumptions, and motivational forces the others have required. Such a quick tour of the field enables the reader to begin a second look at the theoretical assumptions on which clinical work is based. In our seminar, we then reread such psychiatric theorists of family therapy as Boszormenyi-Nagy,[13,14] Laing,[38] and Dicks[19] with the recognition that their task of building a bridge between the theories of individual and social function has only begun.

SCIENTIFIC BASIS

We thought we ought to ask a somewhat naïve question: How much "scientific evidence" was there that "family factors," in fact, could be viewed as "etiologic agents" in the production of "mental illness"? We chose what we felt was the better studies representing the clinical, epidemiologic, field, and laboratory approaches to this knotty problem.

One of the most interesting clinical descriptions of a family is to be found in

Freud's case of Dora.[24,25] The correlation between family circumstances and Dora's symptoms is elegantly demonstrated. Historically, the significance of this case is, of course, the discovery of the importance of infantile sexuality, the function of dreams and intrapsychic factors in general. In fact, Freud's elucidation of Dora's complicity in the family system due to her Oedipal and unconscious homosexual wishes reflects the present-day family systems view of the necessary collusion of all the members of any system to keep it going. The case lent itself beautifully to the age-old question of "whether it is in our-selves or in our stars that we are underlings." The relative significance of constitution, infantile experiences, and current social forces in the etiology of mental illness (hysteria in this case) were again considered.

Other psychoanalytic writers such as Main,[40] and Johnson and Szurek[36] afforded a view of what additional theory is required by the shift to working concurrently (though not conjointly) with the relatives of the identified patient.

With the work of Thomas, Chess, and Birch[59] we returned to the interplay, over time, of temperament and environment in a more systematic, although still primarily clinical, study. Problems of sampling, clinical biases, and interpretation of results were explored in greater detail. This book, by reemphasizing temperament, helps to shift the balance in the nature–nurture controversy away from the preponderant environmentalist bias of American culture and social science. It is a kind of scientific pacifier for a guilt-ridden parental generation tired of being blamed for all their children's ills.

We turned from these clinical impressions to read some material describing attempts at objective specification of the experience aspect of the temperament-experience interaction. We considered hard data such as family structure,[23] paternal absence,[5] or maternal death,[8] and soft data such as Cheek's characterization of the mothers and fathers of schizophrenics.[17,18] Most of the studies could be seriously faulted for their methodology. Even the best, such as Wynne and Singer's studies[68,69] of the parental contribution to thought disorder in schizophrenia, were unsatisfying in the sense that they all seemed to represent such a small piece of the clinical picture. Wender's paper, "On Necessary and Sufficient Conditions in Psychiatric Explanation,"[61] summed up this problem quite well: The examination of single variables as partial causes of an event that occurs rarely and has many causes will yield a very low predictive grasp on the event, even though it has a high level of statistical significance. Wender's own review of the genetic studies of schizophrenia, the most convincing paper we could find on the temperament aspect of the formula, suffers from the same difficulty.[62]

At this point, we abandoned the medical model of first diagnosing a sick or deviant patient and then seeking the etiologic cause in his family. We assembled several papers that could be read as descriptions of the activity of the family as a disordered or malfunctioning group: Ravich,[47] Bauman and Roman,[9] and Reiss.[48] We then looked upon the Wynne and Singer, Reiss, and Cheek papers and viewed them in the same light. From this standpoint, the family can be seen as setting out to accomplish a task (provided either by life or by the experimenter) and doing it well or badly. The trouble they are having with it appears to be strikingly the same in each study: They are spending time managing their relations with each other rather than thinking about the task. Once that point of view had been reached, we were ready to appreciate work such as Scheflen's on the ethology of the family as an interactive group.[56]

THERAPY

Having surveyed available theories of the family, and the question of "scientific evidence," one can read better the writings of the major family therapists and compare them with films or videotapes of their work.[1,3,15,16,28,33–35,42,45,46,54,55,63–68,70]

We tried to appreciate what each of the therapists was trying to accomplish and to identify the special techniques used to get that result. In this way, we concentrated on the unique characteristics of each one, their philosophy, personality, and tactics, rather than on what they all have in common. It is difficult to abstract a useful general theory or description of family therapy from the literature (see Beels and Ferber, "Family Therapy: A View,"[10] for one such attempt). The most important benefit that can be gained from reading the literature of family therapy is to secure a collection of models and scenarios from which the student chooses the most appropriate for himself and the family he is treating.

CONCLUSION

Although this volume is entitled a "primer" in family therapy, this article has referred very little to literature on techniques. This is due partly to the fact that the technical aspects of all therapies tend to be less written about than more theoretical considerations. The newness of the field also contributes to this problem, but of much greater significance is the substantial increase in the role of direct observation of therapy by the use of videotape, one-way screens, films, audiotapes, and live supervision. The impact of these nonliterary methods are substantial and will in many ways guide future theoretic advances. The role, for example, of varying types of feedback in social systems and the very profound, heretofore neglected, role of nonverbal communications are already shaping theoretic advances. These technologic advances have already played and will continue to play a role in the teaching and practice of family therapy. The hard work of sorting out the wheat from the chaff in this technologic explosion remains ahead of us.

Meanwhile, the reading of both technical and literary works remains a time-tested medium for deepening our appreciation of the complexities before us. Hopefully, as "cool media," they will restrain our overzealous attempts to change and modify human behavior before we understand more fully either ourselves or the multiple forces impinging upon us.

REFERENCES

1. Ackerman, NW: Movie of Hillcrest Family (obtainable through Psychological Cinema Register, Pennsylvania State University, University Park, Pa)

2. Ackerman, NW (ed): Family Process. New York, Basic Books, 1970

3. Ackerman, NW: Treating the Troubled Family (chapters containing interview transcripts). New York, Basic Books, 1966

4. Albee E: Who's Afraid of Virginia Woolf? New York, Atheneum, 1962

5. Anderson R: Where's Dad? Arch Gen Psychiatry 18:641–649, 1968

6. Aries P: Centuries of Childhood, A So-

cial History of Family. New York, Vintage Books, 1962

7. Austen J: Pride and Prejudice.

8. Barry H Jr, Lindemann E: Critical ages for maternal bereavement in psychoneurosis. Psychosom Med 22:166–181, 1968

9. Bauman G, Roman M: Interaction testing in the study of marital dominance. Fam Process 5:230–242, 1966

10. Beels CC, Ferber A: Family therapy: A view. Fam Process 8:280–318, 1969

11. Book of Genesis, I:28

12. Blum H: A psychoanalytic view of *Who's Afraid of Virginia Woolf?*. J Am Psychoanal Assoc 17:888–903, 1969

13. Boszormenyi-Nagy I: A theory of relationships, experience and transaction, in Boszormenyi-Nagy I, Framo J (eds): Intensive Family Therapy. New York, Harper & Row, 1965, chap 2

14. Boszormenyi-Nagy I: Intensive family therapy as process, in Boszormenyi-Nagy I, Framo J (eds): Intensive Family Therapy. New York, Harper & Row, 1965, chap 3

15. Bowen M: The use of family theory in clinical practice. Compr Psychiatry 7:345–374, 1966

16. Bowen videotapes (obtainable through Dr. Murray Bowen, Department of Psychiatry, Medical College of Virginia, Richmond, Va)

17. Cheek F: The father of the schizophrenic. Arch Gen Psychiatry 13:336–345, 1965

18. Cheek F: Schizophrenic mothers in word and deed. Fam Process 3:155–177, 1964

19. Dicks H: Marital Tensions. New York, Basic Books, 1967

20. Eliot TS: The Cocktail Party. New York, Harcourt Brace, 1950

21. Ellenberger H: The Discovery of the Unconscious. New York, Basic Books, 1970

22. Ferber A, Mendelsohn M, Napier A (eds): The Book of Family Therapy. New York, Science House, 1972

23. Ferber A, Kliger D, Zwerling I, et al: Current family structure: Psychiatric emergencies and patient fate. Arch Gen Psychiatry 16:659–667, 1967

24. Freud S: The clinical picture, in A Case of Hysteria, vol 7 (standard ed). London, Hogarth, pp 15–63

25. Freud S: Postscript, in A Case of Hysteria, vol 7 (standard ed). London, Hogarth, pp 112–122

26. Glick ID, Haley J: Family Therapy and Research. New York, Grune & Stratton, 1971

27. Goodall J: In the Shadow of Man. Boston, Houghton-Mifflin, 1971

28. Haley J: Strategies of Psychotherapy. New York, Grune & Stratton, 1963, chaps 6, 7

29. Haley J: Toward a theory of pathological families, in Boszormenyi-Nagy I, Zuk G (eds): Family Therapy and Disturbed Families. Palo Alto, Calif, Science and Behavior Books, 1967

30. Haley J (ed): Changing Families: A Family Therapy Reader. New York, Grune & Stratton, 1971

31. Howells JG: The Theory and Practice of Family Psychiatry. New York, Brunner-Mazel, 1971

32. Jackson D: The study of the family. Fam. Process 4:1, 1965

33. Jackson D, Weakland J: Conjoint family therapy. Some considerations on theory, technique and results. Psychiatry 24:30–45, 1961

34. Jackson D, Weakland J: Movie of the Hillcrest Family (obtainable through Psychological Cinema Register, Pennsylvania State University, University Park, Pa)

35. Jackson D, Weakland J, Yalom I: An example of family homeostasis and patient change, in Masserman J (ed): Current Psychiatric Therapies, vol. 4. New York, Grune & Stratton, 1964

36. Johnson A, Szurek SA: The genesis of antisocial acting out in children and adults. Psycholanal Q 21:323–343, 1952

37. LaBarre W: The Ghost Dance. New York, Doubleday, 1970.

38. Laing RD: Individual and family structure, in Lomas P (ed): The Predicament of the Family. London, Hogarth, 1967

39. Levi-Strauss C: The family, in Shapiro HL (ed): Man, Culture, and Society. London, Oxford Univ Pr, 1967, chap 12

40. Main TF: Mutual projection in a marriage. Compr Psychiatry 7:432–439, 1966

41. Mead M: Sex, Temperament. New York, Dell, 1900, chaps 17,18

42. Minuchin S, Montalvo B, Guerney B, et al: Families of the Slums. New York, Basic Books, 1967

43. Parsons T: The American family—Its relations to personality and to the social structure, in Parsons T, Bales RF (eds): Family Socialization and Interaction Process. Glencoe, Ill, Free Press, 1955, chap 1

44. Parsons T: Family structure and the socialization of the child, in Parsons T, Bales RF (eds): Family Socialization and Interaction Process. Glencoe, Ill, Free Press, 1955, chap 2

45. Paul N: The role of mourning and empathy in conjoint marital therapy, in Zuk G, Boszormenyi-Nagy I (eds): Family Therapy and

Disturbed Families. Palo Alto, Calif, Science and Behavior Books, 1967

46. Paul N, Grosser G: Operational mourning and its role in conjoint family therapy. Community Ment Health J 1:339–345, 1965

47. Ravich RA: The use of an interpersonal game-test in conjoint marital psychotherapy. Am J Psychother 23:217–229, 1969

48. Reiss D: Individual thinking and family interaction. Arch Gen Psychiatry 5:80–93, 1967

49. Rieff P: The Triumph of the Therapeutic. New York, Harper & Row, 1966, p 26

50. Sager CT, Kaplan HS (eds): Progress in Group and Family Therapy. New York Brunner-Mazel, 1972

51. Sander F: Family therapy or religion: A re-reading of T.S. Eliot's *The Cocktail Party.* Fam Process 9:279–296, 1970

52. Sander F: Some thoughts on Thomas Szasz. Am J Psychol 125:135–137, 1969

53. Sander F, Beels C, Christian A: A didactic course for family therapy trainees. Fam Process 9:411–423. 1970

54. Satir V: Conjoint Family Therapy. Palo Alto, Calif, Science and Behavior Books, 1964

55. Schaffer L, Wynne L, Day J, et al: On the nature and sources of the psychiatrist's experience with the family of the schizophrenic. Psychiatry 25:23–45, 1962

56. Scheflen A: Human communication: Behavioral programs and their integration in interaction. Behav Sci 13:44–55, 1968

57. Skolnick AS, Skolnick JH: Family in Transition. Boston, Little, Brown, 1971

58. Szasz T: The Myth of Mental Illness. New York, Harper & Row, 1961

59. Thomas A, Chess S, Birch H: Temperament and Behavior Disorder in Children. New York, New York University Press, 1963

60. Watzlawick P, Beavin J, Jackson DD: The Pragmatics of Human Communications. New York, Norton, 1967

61. Wender P: On necessary and sufficient conditions in psychiatric explanation. Arch Gen Psychiatry 16:41–47, 1967

62. Wender P: The role of genetics in the etiology of the schizophrenias. Am J Orthopsychiatry 39:447–458, 1969

63. Whitaker C: Movie of Hillcrest Family (obtainable through Psychological Cinema Register, Pennsylvania State University, University Park, Pa)

64. Whitaker C: Psychotherapy with couples. Am J Psychother 12:18–23, 1958

65. Whitaker C: Acting out in family psychotherapy, in Abt LE, Weismann SL (eds): Acting Out—Theoretical and Clinical Aspects. New York, Grune & Stratton, 1965

66. Wynne L: Some indications and contraindications for exploring family therapy, in Boszormenyi-Nagy I, Framo J (eds): Intensive Family Therapy. New York, Harper & Row, 1965

67. Wynne L: The study of intrafamilial alignments and splits in exploratory family therapy, in Ackerman NW, Beatman F, Sherman S (eds): Exploring the Base for Family Therapy. New York, Family Service Association, 1961

68. Wynne L, Singer MT: Thought disorder and family relations of schizophrenics. Parts I, II. Arch Gen Psychiatry 9:191–206, 1963

69. Wynne L, Singer MT: Thought disorder and family relations of schizophrenics. Parts III, IV. Arch Gen Psychiatry 12:186–212, 1965

70. Zuk G: Family Therapy: A Triadic Approach. New York, Behavioral Publications, Inc., 1971

A Standard Initial Interview

Paul Franklin, M.D. and Phoebe Prosky, M.S.W.

A FAMILY SYSTEMS interviewing format is particularly useful in mental health consultation. It can serve effectively as a diagnostic tool and for planning and initiating psychotherapy of any variety. In routinely seeing whole family groups for initial evaluation, one may considerably improve the effectiveness and economy of clinical work, even in instances where family therapy as such is not contemplated. Information is developed rapidly and in appropriate multi-dimensional complexity; scapegoating of the identified patient is reduced; family systems resistances are made visible, and strategies for coping with them are initiated from the outset (the premature termination of apparently successful psychotherapy often relates to stress placed on the family system by favorable changes in the identified patient with family resistance to those changes). While it is not always practical or psychologically feasible to arrange for such family consultations, substantial benefits can accrue to the patient, his family, and the therapeutic enterprise when this procedure is used.

The psychotherapist accustomed to one-to-one dyadic interviewing is apt to feel bewildered by the rate and volume of information obtained. We will attempt here to provide a simple guide to considering such a consultation. We speak of "a" standard initial family interview; it would be presumptuous to suggest there is *one* correct way to carry out such a consultation. While some regularization of interviewing technique is possible, and major training centers tend to teach in fairly standard ways, there is obviously much difference as well, the most obvious sources of which are the family itself, and the personal style, training, and theoretical persuasion of the therapist.

An overall statement of the purposes of an initial family systems consultation would certainly include all of those conventionally associated with mental health evaluations: assessment of an individual family member's psychic functioning, principle conflictual areas, adaptive, and coping capabilities, biologic endowment, skill levels, and so on.

There are additional goals of the *family* consultation which are distinctive to it:

Mapping the systems aspects of the presenting complaint. In this regard one must begin constructing from the first moment of engagement, a multi-generational map of the family, which includes a time dimension. In this sense, it is a focused historical review that takes into account the bio-psycho-social development of individuals, of dyads such as the marital pair, of generations, and of the entire family. To the degree that this is crisis oriented (see Pittman), the map will deliberately be limited to defining those aspects of the system relevant to the immediate presenting difficulty; where growth and rehabilitative goals exist, more extensive maps need to be constructed. Structures to be mapped

---

Reprint requests should be addressed to Paul Franklin, M.D., 11 Riverside Drive, New York, N.Y. 10023.

should not be limited to the nuclear family or even the extended kin network but must include all of the relevant natural systems: school, work, government, with which the family system is involved to the degree that transactions across these interfaces bear on the issues being dealt with.

(1) Mapping of family systems resistance processes and (2) therapeutic interference with them. Perhaps this may be spoken of as the establishment of a therapeutic presence. From the outset, an attempt will be made to weave the therapist into the family's defensive social patterns. Bafflement, scapegoating, obsessive undoing, segregation of affect, maintenance of family secrets and myths, collusive hypocrisy and deceit, schizmatic alliances, and other such systems equilibrators are all potentially operative. Indeed, they may often be expressed in the behaviors known as psychiatric symptoms.

In this respect the consultation situation is exactly analogous to that pertaining in dyadic interactions: there may be no doubt at all about the seriousness and validity of the patient's wish for growth and relief from distress, yet it would be naïve to fail to recognize that resistances and defenses are inevitably present. Homeostatic equilibria are maintained at the level of individual psychology as well as at the level of the family system. Thus, the family system, like the individual, strives both for change and stability (morphogenesis and morphostasis).

The initial interview has all the earmarks of a *shiddoch**—with all the excitement, uncertainty, newness, and difficulty of understanding. Two parties come together by previous arrangement, and they meet for the first time in the knowledge that they will need to find a way to work and live together. Thus, family therapy begins almost as a marriage between the family and the therapist.

During the initial interview, the tentative establishment of an emotional contact between the therapist and the various members of the family takes place. They appraise the therapist and his skill, as well as his capacity to understand them and to relate to their distress. In turn, the therapist appraises the family in toto as well as its various members. He evaluates the pathology as well as the healthy aspects of their relationships. He listens with an ear to intergenerational issues, noticing how family patterns appear through the generations. After a tentative diagnosis is established, the therapist identifies some of the outstanding conflicts and shares his observations with the family. This leads to the beginning of the therapeutic contract.

Treatment goals and prognosis (hopefully recorded) should be set by the end of the initial consultation: There should be some indication as to what the therapist and family as a system wish to work on and a tentative estimate of the prospects for a favorable outcome.

It is important from the onset to conceive of the consultation as the first *two* interviews of the work. The first meeting will usually be so colored by the qualities peculiar to a new experience that it is essential to see the family a second time to allow for the more correct appraisal of aspects which may have been exaggerated or underplayed in the initial contact. In this paper, we will

---

*Yiddish for "an arranged marriage."

touch on: (1) initial contact with the family; (2) the family concept and handling resistances to it; (3) office arrangements; (4) the first moments of meeting; (5) conducting the interview; (6) a note of family history-taking; (7) the second interview; and (8) therapeutic planning and the contract.

The Initial Contact

Family therapy begins at the first moment of the therapist's telephone contact with a family. In contrast to individual therapy, the therapist is often called on to make a pronounced intervention at as early a time as the initial telephone call from the person requesting help. It is in this conversation that the therapist *sets the ground rules for a family system approach.* The family member making the contact will frequently define the problem as involving one person (usually a child) or only one part of the family (the marital pair, most often). The therapist must then begin the mapping process by finding out who else is in the family system. By "family" here, we mean to include all persons with strong reciprocal emotional ties who have a current or historical relevance to the problem. This is most often the nuclear family but may also include such others as grandparents, friends, housekeepers, and sometimes even pets (see Napier).

Our practice is to answer all incoming telephone calls ourselves. If the occasion does not permit a telephone review of the problem and a canvas of family membership, we set aside another time for doing this by appointment.

The family group, as defined in this initial telephone conversation is the one the therapist will want to see. Flexibility is called for: In one situation a delinquent adolescent flatly refused to attend sessions until a friend of his was allowed to sit in and participate in the treatment process. He continued to bring his friend for several sessions until he was reassured that the therapist was not going to scapegoat him.

Resistance to the Family Concept

Sometimes, the family refuses to involve one or more of its members. In such instances, it is often useful for the therapist to review his own doubts and anxieties: Is he convinced that the whole family need be present at the session? Beginning therapists often have a fear of dealing with so many people, of exposing the children to the affairs of their parents, of handling an explosive marital situation with both partners present, etc. If the therapist has such resistance, it is highly likely that it will reinforce resistance in the family. One approach to the telephone initiation of the family into family therapy, and one that is very useful to the beginner in the field, is simply to maintain as policy that if the therapist is to see the family, they must all be there. This apparently uncompromising approach is often effective in achieving compliance. It usually proves futile for the therapist himself to speak to the reluctant family member, because by so doing, he is allying himself with the initiator of the contact, thereby antagonizing other members. Moreover, his unnecessary participation prevents him from recognizing the source of the resistance.

Initiation of family sessions with only part of the family present is risky. Many experienced therapists have come to regard the willingness of the entire family to participate as an important prognostic sign. Should the therapist ally himself with part of the family, it undoubtedly threatens the rest. A woman called, asking for help in solving a conflict with her mother. Upon her urging, the therapist agreed to see her alone first. During the later therapy an impasse occurred inasmuch as the woman was furious with the therapist for not allying himself with her viewpoint. She said, "I purposely saw you first. I wanted you to understand how I felt. And now you're completely ignoring it." Here her intention was to turn the therapist into her protector before confronting her mother, which in turn would surely have alienated the mother.

Even experienced family interviewers are repeatedly surprised at the difficulties in assessing family life and its psychopathology in the absence of all of its members. Resistance to family sessions can take many forms, the most frequent being the protest that *another* family member objects. Thus, in the initial telephone call, the therapist should ask if other family members are aware of the call and how they feel about it.

One woman insisted that her husband would not participate in a family session. When the therapist asked if she had discussed it with him, it turned out that she had never mentioned it. At the very least, the woman was collusive in excluding her husband. In another instance, a mother telephoned concerning her delinquent adolescent daughter. She insisted, however, that her daughter would not come in for sessions. When the therapist asked why not, the woman said her daughter did not believe in psychotherapy. In response to the further question, "Who else in your family feels that way?", the woman began to talk of her own bad experiences in therapy and revealed that she was calling at her husband's insistence and *against her own will.* Here we see the child's acting out as a device that both expresses and hides the parental conflict and resistance. This pattern was quickly brought to light by a family approach to the telephone call. The resistant member is rarely isolated in his lack of motivation. His attitude is often shared by one or more other members.

Office Arrangements

The office should be large enough to hold the family group and allow for free movement: One member may want to pace the floor or remove himself from the immediate context of the family, or a child might need to hide behind the desk. There may be more chairs than the number of people expected so as to permit the family to represent their structural relationship by the seating arrangements. Important functional subgroupings of members may be indicated, for example by leaving an empty chair at an important point in their spatial configuration. To highlight this process, some clinicians prefer to provide exactly as many chairs as are needed for the family plus the therapist (s). They permit the family to enter the interviewing room first and to arrange themselves before he enters. This is frequently a valuable guide to family splits, and to the position (spatially represented) the therapist is intended to occupy. In a case where the space left for the therapist is in the middle of the family, it may serve as an indication that there are two warring factions that are trying to trap him in the middle. It is usually advisable for the therapist to rearrange the seating positions so as to extricate himself from this "trap." Generally, he will find it most convenient to sit where he can see all members at a glance.

A mother flanked by her two sons left a chair empty for the therapist between this group and another made up of her husband and daughter. Before seating himself, the therapist noticed the arrangement, to which the mother replied, "That's the way it always is." In a moment, there was an active discussion of the split in the family and of the hope the therapist would both maintain it and help bridge it.

If possible, an adult should be available in the waiting room to supervise young children should the therapist want to excuse them for a short period of time. The therapist may at the very least wish to have a tape recorder available to review aspects of the transaction with the family. Video equipment is frequently used as well (see Alger).

The First Moments of Meeting

At times, the family members present themselves at the office one or two at a time. Even if the last members are quite late in arriving, it is advisable to follow through with the thrust of the telephone agreement and await to begin the session until all are present. At a later point in therapy, this same situation will have a variety of meanings in the context of the work, and the decision to start or wait for all members will have to be made based on the current meaning; but it is well at first to wait for all to be present.

Sometimes, on arrival, the family confronts the therapist with the information that one member will not be present. This bodes ill for the work. Generally at this point, the session should take place anyway, but the therapist during the course of the hour should explore thoroughly with the family why the missing member is absent with a full explanation as to whom among those present is collusive in keeping him out, if this can be ascertained.

The therapist should make it clear that the absence of a member may be a reflection of another member's emotional needs; where this can be established, he will usually do best to encourage *this* member of the family to bring the person in for the next session. A chair may be left empty in the circle of seating to symbolically include the absent member and indirectly indicate that absence will not be accepted by the therapist.

In one instance, the husband was only too eager to accept the flimsy excuse of his wife for not coming in. He wanted to talk privately to the therapist to express his belief that his absent wife was engaged in an adulterous relationship. Private sharing between therapist and one family member of such "secrets" is very hazardous. The secret becomes coercive, severely limiting communication at later points in time. Many experienced therapists explicitly state that they will not keep secrets; information that must remain private should be kept so from the onset.

Visual data collecting about the family begins as soon as the therapist sets eyes on them. How are they dressed? How do they hold themselves? Who is alone and who clings to whom? The therapist should particularly notice any differences in the family between how they interact in the waiting room as contrasted with their presentation of themselves in the consultation room; do they talk naturally to each other while waiting for the session to begin or are they frightened, fragmented or subdued.

The family's way of greeting the therapist can be quite important. Who stands up first, speaks first, dresses, scolds, or huddles with the children? In one family where the presenting complaint concerned excessive and frequent urination in an adolescent girl, the mother darted into the bathroom as the family began to leave the waiting room with the therapist to move into the consultation room. Her ambivalent tie to, and identification with the index patient was suggested by this first quick action. Its elucidation was the key to a successful therapeutic venture.

It is good policy to shake hands with each family member, particularly the children. Much is told in the character of a handshake. More importantly, by touching each person, even the smallest child, and acknowledging them, their importance for the work at hand is signified and their individuality recognized as well.

Overall mood as well as affective subgroupings as evidenced by verbal and nonverbal exchanges and similarities of appearance are important. In one family, consisting of mother, father, and two children, it was striking to notice the similarity in appearance and facial expression of the father and older son, who appeared to be depressed and subdued, as contrasted with the mother and younger son who evidenced great spontaneity in facial expression and body movements. These parents had each had a former marriage of which these children were products; the affective polarization noted here represented both their principal reason for choosing each other as mates as well as the dominant problem in the relationship.

Conducting the Interview

Everyone is seated. The therapist may find himself among a quiet, uncomfortable group of people he does not know. After a brief silence, he may appropriately relate himself to the family's feeling of fright and discomfort, perhaps by saying, "You look uneasy here. I feel uneasy, too, not knowing anything about you and your situation." The family may then begin to talk about their attitude toward being in the session. It is often useful for the therapist to begin the session by noting his observations of nonverbal aspects of family interaction already observed. This has the advantage of immediately establishing the relevance of nonverbal communication. It may also interfere with a major defensive mode before that is frozen. In the family just described, he might note, "You two, father and son, seem to be unhappy, while you others, mother and son, look quite cheerful." In another instance, the therapist might note to the family that the children seem quite frightened, while the father appears unconcerned and detached. This may provide a very good opening for the therapist to ask various family members what they were told about coming to the session. An ordinarily lively child may seem inexplicably withdrawn in an interview if the therapist does not know the child was coerced into coming with the unnecessary agreement he did not have to talk. (Such a child will delightedly reveal valuable information but can be maneuvered into silence by such a parental ruse.)

Family History-taking

Taking a family history is distinctive in at least one important way. It aims to elucidate the Rashomon effect, to emphasize the multiple interlocking perspectives that contribute to the perceptual–action–cognitive matrix that *is* the life of the family. The search for reality is abandoned before it begins in the recognition that history is constantly being rewritten for all living organisms, that the mapping process is an action in its own right. Recognizing this leads, in our hands at least, to a style that depends much more on investigations of affectively intense issues and themes rather than on a systematic inventory of classes of experience or information. History-taking in this sense is very much a part of the living therapeutic engagement; interpretations in words or actions are made early on and history-taking is tied to the strands of memory thus activated. We do not mean that a conceptual structure does not exist for the therapist. As we noted in our introduction, his goal is to make a multi-dimensional, developmental map of the generational structure of the family. To do this in a way that is emotionally valid requires that he attend to the immediately presenting affective issues, else he will be obsessively, but meaninglessly, penciling in information in categories of little or no consequence for the family.

In a traditional setting, the therapist's first order of business may be to take a formal history of the identified patient. In family therapy, this is not the case. The therapist begins by observing the dynamic interplay among the family members and uses this to gradually enlarge his perception past and present of the family life. The family history emerges over the course of therapy as it has relation to current family emotional configurations.

In one instance, the therapist commented on the isolation and withdrawal of the father in the family setting. The father responded that for as long as he could remember, he had felt as though he were a loner. At this point the therapist encouraged him to speak about his past experiences as they related to this problem. In this way, the therapist connected the present with the past in a living context that had current emotional meaning for the family. The historical material came alive and had emotional impact. This approach also elicits lively family participation in the context of history: In the instance cited, the therapist noticed the wife had tears in her eyes as the husband was speaking; when he commented about this, she began to talk about her own feeling of isolation as a child and how awful that felt to her. The function of establishing ties between family members on the basis of common experiences in their backgrounds and their empathy for each other was served as well.

This approach to history is important from yet another standpoint. As already noted, memory changes in accordance with the present situation. In the example above, as the man who was so isolated was able to establish an emotional link with his wife and with the therapist and as he felt less isolated, new historical material appeared: rather than seeing himself completely alone in the backyard as a child, he began to recall several "forgotten" memories of childhood playmates and playing games with other children. The beginning family therapist often feels it necessary to collect as much historical data as possible in order to make an appropriate intervention. This is not the case; only focused, intense, relevant, affectively alive, yet circumscribed, history-taking is therapeutically useful.

The Second Interview

We feel that the picture that emerges is not conclusive without a second interview with the family. When the family first comes to the therapist, they are naturally anxious and feel constricted in the unfamiliar situation. In a second interview, they do not face the unknown and are often more relaxed, allowing the therapist to elicit additional nuances and dimensions of their interaction and thus gain a deeper understanding of the family as a system.

The second interview is not simply for the purpose of gathering more details of family life. It is to help the therapist to feel the family qualities in a more relaxed situation. In reviewing his observations, he must be careful to include his internal responses to the family, as these are as important in helping him to formulate the issues as are the cues that come to him from outside.

Therapeutic Planning and the Contract

Most families come into the therapeutic situation with a knowledge of their symptoms, but they have no idea of what the underlying causes of their distress are. At the end of the second interview, the therapist should share his tentative formulations with them—both their difficulties and their strengths—along with the direction of his plans for therapeutic intervention.

A critical decision ordinarily made at this point is what persons should be directly involved in the therapeutic venture. Family systems concepts of treatment will apply at all times, but the actual persons involved in the work will reflect the needs and capacities of the family system as well as the preferences and capabilities of the therapist. This may mean the family's adding important people who have not yet been a part of the work, or sometimes, as in the case of young children, excusing them from regular participation in the sessions. This move may sometimes even lead to eliminating the identified patient from the immediate ongoing work. One family consulted a family therapist about the unruly, rebellious, defiant behavior of their only child, a boy of eight, who was acting out at home and in school. During the consultation, a smoldering conflict erupted between the passive father and the openly belligerent, aggressive wife. The husband at home felt incapable of dealing with her and therefore retreated into his work. In addition, he would go bowling daily with "the boys." When he would come home at 3 a.m., he would find his son sleeping in the bed with his wife.

It seemed clear the boy was a stand-in for his father, and the unexpressed rage that the wife experienced was directed towards the boy. The therapist determined that it would be most productive to work with the couple alone initially on their marital difficulties, and, after a short period, excused the child from the sessions. Inasmuch as the conflict was put in its proper focus and the scapegoating was relieved, the child showed remarkable spontaneous abatement of his symptoms after only a few sessions with the husband and wife.

It is inappropriate to attempt to review here the wide range of considerations entering into treatment planning. It is important, though, for the busy therapist to recognize that to do this adequately takes time. However it may be constructed, it is obviously desirable for the treatment contract to be clearly spelled out and reviewed in sufficient detail so that family members and the therapist understand what is being proposed and how this grows out of the experience they have had in the course of the initial consultation with each other.

The Clinical Home Visit

Donald A. Bloch, M.D.

O NE MAY THINK of the chairs, couches, beds, pictures, books, toys, kitchen equipment, personal clothing, drugs, and other multitudinous artifacts of a family's daily life as art materials. The physical and social space available for their use and display is a multi-dimensional canvas on which the family represents its structure, its inner world. The physical household, its contents, and the social arrangements for their use are a vast, living, and changing representation of the psycho-social life of the family and can be entered into, and joined with, by the clinician in such a way as to complexly reveal the forces operating in the family system.

At any point in time, the creation, never static, resolves, integrates, and expresses the inner and outer world of its systems creators. What materials are available, what cultural metaphors, what constraints? Is the family rich or poor, city or country? The household, like all such creations, but more intensely so, is interactive. It too is participant, setting not only a stage for the human drama that unfolds within it, but, in its turn, molding and modifying, limiting and enhancing its creators, the family.

We shall for convenience speak of this physical complex and the social patterns of its use as "the home." To enter into it professionally for an hour or two, or a day or two, or longer, is to make a "clinical home visit." The purposes of such a visit are both diagnostic and therapeutic for the family therapist. This article will discuss how to conduct such a visit and how to make clinical use of it.

Introducing the clinical home visit to the family can be done quite simply at the point where the initial family orientation is being established. Some such language as this may be appropriate: "In the course of coming to know you as a family, I would like to meet with you in your own home. This will give me a better understanding of how life is for you in the ordinary course of events." Or, "In addition to seeing you together in my office, I will want to have a chance to visit with you in your own home. We can make arrangements for that to suit your convenience and mine." Said simply, there is an intuitive natural understanding of this on the part of families. They know they are different on their home ground, and that this is a difference with meaning for the life of the family, and may be related to the issues bringing them for assistance. *The clinical home visit feels comfortable and natural to families and, in my experience, the suggestion for the visit is always accepted.*

It should be noted at the outset that the visit is a professional event, not a social one, and, among other things, *a fee should be charged.* It is important to emphasize that the purpose of the visit is to advance the therapeutic work. While this is not intended to introduce a note of excessive formality into the

Reprint requests should be addressed to Donald A. Bloch, M.D., Nathan W. Ackerman Family Institute, Inc., 149 E. 78 Street, New York, N.Y. 10021.

© *1973 by Grune & Stratton, Inc.*

proceedings, it does permit certain important activities to take place, which might not be possible otherwise. Included on the list of such important but socially difficult activities is the full exploration and tour of the house from top to bottom, which includes access to areas not ordinarily publicly open.

The professional nature of the visit can be underscored by the manner of the clinician in his bearing and his attitude; he can, in a dignified yet warm way take charge of the proceedings. There is indeed a flow of adaptation from therapist to family in both directions. By monitoring this mutual adaptation, the therapist can come to learn much useful information about his own reactions to the family as well as about significant coping styles they have.

While we emphasize the professional nature of the visit, this should not speak for excessive formality, nor should one allow oneself to be held in the role of distinguished visitor and limited to public areas and public interactions. It often is appropriate to think of oneself as an old family friend, or favorite aunt or uncle, privy to the secrets of the family and to the private spaces, yet with some degree of distance in regard to its more intense emotional interactions. Depending upon the sex of the visitor, it is possible to help with child care, making drinks, playing with the children. Most often, it is desirable to have a male-female co-therapy team make the home visit, since this provides an opportunity for easy involvement with the male and female sides of family life. If this is not practical, however, it is possible to cultivate the opposite sex sides of oneself so as to allow for a comparatively easy involvement in all areas.

In middle class families, the most convenient time and format for a clinical home visit is in the late afternoon continuing through the dinner hour and into the early evening. Ordinarily, this is the one time of the day when the entire family is expected to be at home; indeed, one can insist on making the visit at a time and on a day when this will be so. Food preparation, the arrival of older school children and working members of the household, the conversation around the dinner table all provide excellent natural occasions for observing important family interaction.

Dinner hour is not necessarily the best time to visit families from other socioeconomic classes. Our experience, for example, with poor inner-city families has led us to choose the late morning for families with pre-school children, and the immediate post-school time for those with older children. In these families dinner hour may not exist, or may be quite unstructured. Food may be served continuously throughout the day on an individual basis; the responsibility for providing a meal for a professional stranger may be vastly more heavy than the social system can reasonably bear. This is not necessarily so; a prudent and respectful attitude will permit other possibilities to develop.

> Home visits were being made regularly to a black inner-city family, consisting of a grandmother, her daughter, two granddaughters, and a great-granddaughter and grandson, all living on welfare in a three-room apartment. Careful negotiation of the issue of feeding the therapist took some weeks; his tastes were assessed, particularly in regard to his tolerance for foods unfamiliar to him. Following this courtship, he was treated to delicious servings of foods strange to him. This act of caring for the therapist helped to reduce the sense of awe, strangeness, and distance between a white, middle-class male and the black, predominantly female lower-class family.

The family sets the tone and pace of the visits with facilitating suggestions from the therapist. It is necessary for him to indicate quite directly that his interest is in being with them in the way which is most comfortable for them, that he need not be treated specially, and that he has the capacity for enjoying the family on its own terms.

> A clinical family home visit was being made to a wealthy family in a fashionable suburban area. The visit was to last for 2 days. The team making the visit consisted of the family therapist and a psychoanalyst treating one member of the family. Immediately after arrival, hors d'oeuvres and drinks were served, both in profusion. The index patient was a young woman in her twenties, who had failed to mention the alcohol problem of her older brother, a problem that needed no further elaboration with the unfolding of the cocktail hour that evening and the flock of Bloody Marys served for breakfast the next morning.

The clinicians were welcomed into this home by a standard social route, and thus were further privileged to see an aspect of the family's malfunctioning, which had not been known before. *The emotional impact of seeing something first-hand can reveal the nature of events in a way not to be attained otherwise.*

> A co-therapy team made a home visit to the family of the owner of a fashionable New York City restaurant, at which they had both dined. The restaurant owner and his wife lived in a stripped, barren apartment. The table was set with paper placemats and odds and ends of silverware and crockery. No cocktails were offered before dinner; the wine served with dinner was a sweet dessert wine of a very inexpensive variety. The main dish was spaghetti, which had dried out and burned, together with tasteless pork chops. The four children sat at the table and grabbed for chops with their hands. During dinner, the mother did not eat at all, while the father sat fully dressed in his business suit, smiling over the scene. The contrast between his place of business and home could not have been greater.

The first-hand experience of this barren, ungiving, unnourishing dinner table environment provided an orientation to issues of nurturance and mutual support patterns between the parents, which could not have been gained as effectively in any other way. It was not that these events had not been mentioned in the consultation room. Their power, impact, and relative importance could not have been apprehended as easily any other way.

At times, data collected at a home visit require important reassessments of the family.

> During an initial interview where the index patient was a 10-yr-old girl, the parents spoke glancingly of a "suicide gesture" the youngster had made. In discussing it, they indicated that they did not take it seriously, that in fact the "trivial gesture" consisted only of slipping out of a first floor window to the ground below. In the course of a home visit I asked to be shown the specific window where this had taken place. The window lay on a curving wall of the house, with a sheer drop of about eight feet to the sloping ground below. The area below was dark and forbidding; it was impossible to fall into it without being endangered by sharp bushes poking upward. It was difficult to conceive of this as a "trivial" event after having seen the place of its occurrence.

A complete physical examination of the family living space is an essential feature of the clinical visit. It is desirable to make as much of a tour as is possible within the limitations of time available. At the very least, the tour should include a full journey through all of the rooms of the house. Frequently, it is desirable to use a child as a guide, since the conduct of the tour will often include revealing commentary. In any case, no places should be permitted to be off limits and the usual restriction of visitors to public areas does not apply. The intimate areas of the house are related to the therapeutic work in the same way that the intimate areas of the body are routinely examined in a good physical examination, without apology, shame, or prurience. (A small area, often overlooked, yet most usefully looked into, is the medicine cabinet.)

If at all possible, the visit should include a tour of other significant places of family activity, work sites, schools, and former dwellings. Family members enjoy and profit from these tours of the past; they respond favorably to the therapist's interest and to the sense of historical continuity and the flow of family life expressed thereby.

The goal is to map the space in which people live and in which they have lived. In a real sense, this is a journey through time as well as space. One conducts a kind of archeologic investigation.

> A home visit was made with a schizoid young man in his thirties to two cities in the deep South, one in Tennessee, the other in Georgia. In the course of the visit to the home of his 80-yr-old physician father, still actively practicing medicine, we journeyed to the red-dirt Tennessee farm from which his father had originally come, and thus had a chance to experience the origins of the family in post-Civil War time. In Georgia, we visited his older siblings, a full generation older than the patient, to see and partake of the aristocratic life of white Southern professional gentry. Dinner in the parental home was served by the mother and one black woman servant with whom the mother had been bickering for 40 yr. An elaborate formal meal was served in the sibling's home by three uniformed black waitresses and a butler. The index patient has generally been perceived as a played-out end of the road aristocrat, a conception enriched and deepened by this historical tour of the family space.

These tours of the past reactivate memories, often in therapeutically valuable ways.

> Several meetings had already taken place with a family characterized by bitter unremitting generational warfare. Four young adult children kept up a united front of active vitriolic criticism of their parents; the latter, in their own turn, had neither good word nor thought for their offspring. There was no sign of a break in either of these alliances until a family meeting and therapy session was scheduled for the distant city where they had grown up and where the parents still lived. In the parental home, sitting at the dinner table, two of the three sisters fell to arguing and to competing for the mother's attention and affection. Before long, it became possible to activate and reconstruct this rivalrous component concealed until that time by the impenetrable united front.

By mapping the external space, we make a map of the internal space; at times we are able by such direct observation to discern the principal architect, the designer of the family psycho-social space more clearly than we could otherwise. In current vernacular, what trip is the family on, and *whose trip is it?*

> A young man in his early twenties was endlessly and obsessively occupied with questions about differentiating himself from his family, particularly his father. Along with these concerns he was preoccupied with related issues of personal and work identity. A visit to the mountain retreat where the family home and business was located allowed us to tour a resort consisting of two hundred acres of lakes, rolling fields, chalets, outbuildings, lodges, barns, and pastures. This vast enterprise had been purchased and constructed under the driving leadership of the father, whose dream it was to own and manage such an estate. Not only the patient, but his four siblings, their spouses, and his mother, were engaged in staffing the place.

The same point may be made from a quite different direction. We are familiar from the work of such gifted observers as Oscar Lewis with the profound inter-relationship between space availability and utilization and the sexual life, for example, of poor inner-city or rural families. Consider, though, the sexual consequences of the household space arrangements of a divorced woman with three young children. This woman complained, among other things, of her inability to develop an ongoing relationship with a man. She was an attractive professional woman, sexually interested and interesting.

> Visiting her home, one saw two bedrooms across a very small hall from each other. One was hers, the other belonged to the three children. There was an auxiliary bunkbed in her room, which also contained the family television set; the nighttime routine involved the entire family watching TV together in her bedroom. Clearly, there was no room for a man in that bed. On touring the house, we discovered that the living room was completely open to the children's area without any possibility of privacy. The only place allowing for dalliance was the playroom (sic) in the basement, which contained a suitable studio couch. It also contained almost one hundred dolls and an endless number of children's toys. It was easy to guess the effect that all of this might have on a gentleman caller.

The psychotherapeutic importance of this visit lay not so much in the uncovering of new material, as in the shared sense of conviction of the patient and her therapist as to her priorities and intentions.

There may be a vast difference between the public areas of the house and the private areas. A schizophrenic young woman was in treatment in an open hospital. Her parents were divorced; the general sense about the mother with whom this girl was living was of coldness, and inhospitality, covered with a veneer of social ingratiation.

> The home visit was surprising in that the entrance way, living room, and downstairs areas were generally attractive, warm, inviting, with comfortably upholstered furniture, many nicknacks, pictures, objets d'art, and so on. The sense was of a pleasant, bright, attractive, and cheerful home. On visiting the upstairs bedrooms, there was a sharply contrasting, bleak, underfurnished quality; no sense of enclosure or warmth could be obtained. There was minimal furniture, poor lighting, and a general sense of impoverishment. An additional note of interest was the patient's bedroom. This young woman had an older brother whose marriage had been associated in time with the first of her two out-of-wedlock pregnancies, as well as with a period of rapid schizophrenic decompensation. A poignant note was struck by the only decorations in the room, two bridal bouquets from her brother's wedding; one tied to each of the bedposts at the foot of her bed.

A similar experience was associated with the home visit to an alcoholic school teacher, who in her early 60s was about to retire and whose young adult children were making strong moves to disentangle themselves from her dependent alcoholism.

> The public areas of her home were, again, attractive, warm, charming, and clean. Over some protest, her bedroom was visited on the tour of the house. It was as if it were a dark corner of her soul, filled with debris; bottles, litter, an unmade bed, books lying everywhere, mixed up with clothing, memorabilia, and unidentifiable objects.

The conduct of people in the family and their way of relating during the visit may vividly provide essential pieces of information as to the genesis of psychopathology, particularly as to the *weight* of certain factors. In the family referred to earlier, visited by the family therapist and the psychoanalyst, the identified patient, a young woman, had suffered a severe bilateral hearing loss, which was not discovered until she was 5 or 6 yr old. As a youngster, she had had violent temper tantrums throughout her entire childhood, most particularly occurring at the dinner table. As a way of coping with her, she had been put down in the cellar to cool off when she would have these tantrums.

> During our visit, talk at the dinner table was topical, concerned with the business and social life of the family; conversation was rapid, with much overtalking. What was most striking was the difficulty the clinicians had in following the conversation, even though neither had a hearing loss. It was plain that the index patient could not possibly sort out the voices and it was clear that even as a young adult she had stopped listening to some things that could only have bitterly defeated and frustrated her as a child. The temper tantrums of her younger days at the dinner table were not at all hard to understand in the light of this experience.

An important therapeutic move was to point this out to the family at the moment. The analyst, when he became aware of it, noted rather mildly how difficult it was to follow the conversations. With this suggestion there was a notable reduction in guilt on the part of the parents and in the sense of incapacity and frustration on the part of the girl. It was also possible to experiment at that very moment with some different conversational patterns with the result that, at subsequent meals, a genuine effort was made to attend to her hearing difficulties and to shift the pattern of conversation so as to make it more possible for her to be a participant.

The format of psychotherapeutic practice makes home visiting difficult. Office visits are generally scheduled on a regular basis so that it is difficult to free large blocks of time, especially at those hours in which a home visit could be made. The financial realities of psychotherapeutic practice frequently preclude adequate payment for such a large investment of professional effort. At the very least, making a home visit is inconvenient and expensive, and this certainly promotes resistance to doing so on the part of higher status psychotherapists. Despite the difficulties, the rewards are bountiful for diagnostic understanding and for therapy. It is worth overcoming the resistance.

Often this resistance is based on other sorts of reasons than impracticality. In the same way the family is apt to feel more secure on *its* home ground, practitioners are apt to feel more secure in surroundings where, in principle at least, they can control the level, intensity, and affective quality of the interaction. In this respect, it is as much of a hazard for the clinician to leave the safety of his office and expose himself to the family space as it is for the family to come to the office.

Thus, experience in teaching the procedure of the clinical home visit to trainees has indicated the value of insisting on it being carried out. Until the associated apprehension has been faced, and the tremendous clinical value discovered, considerable social support and self-discipline are required to enable one to undertake these procedures. The beginning family therapist should require this of himself routinely, and *without exception*.

SUGGESTED READINGS

1. Behrens M: Brief home visits by the clinic therapist in the treatment of lower-class patients. Am J Psychiatry 124:371–375, 1967

2. Behrens M, Ackerman N: The home visit as an aid in family diagnosis and therapy. Soc Casework 37:11–19, 1956

3. Behrens M, Goldfarb W: A study of patterns of interaction of families of schizophrenic children in residential treatment. Am J Orthopsychiatry 28:300–312, 1958

4. Behrens M, Meyers DI, Goldfarb W, et al: The Henry Ittleson Center Family Interaction Scales. Genet Psychol Monogr 80:203–295, 1969

5. Behrens M, Rosenthal AJ, Chodoff P: Communication in lower class families of schizophrenics. Arch Gen Psychiatry 18:689–696, 1968

6. Behrens M, Sherman A: Observations of family interaction in the home. Am J Orthopsychiatry 29:243–248, 1959

7. Brown BS: Home visiting by psychiatrists. Arch Gen Psychiatry 7:98–107, 1962

8. Fisch R: Home visits in a private psychiatric practice. Fam Process 3:114–126, 1964

9. Friedman, AS: Family therapy as conducted in the home. Fam Process 1:132–140, 1962

10. Henry J: The study of families by naturalistic observation in Cohen IM (ed): Psychiatric Research Report No. 20. Washington, DC, American Psychiatric Association, 1966

11. Henry J: Pathways to Madness. New York, Random House, 1971.

12. Levine R: Treatment in the home. Soc Work 9:19–28, 1964

13. Lewis O: Five Families: Mexican Case Studies in the Culture of Poverty. New York, Basic Books, 1959

14. Manning J, Glasser B: The home visit in the treatment of psychiatric patients awaiting hospitalization. J Health Hum Behav 3:97–104, 1962

15. Morgan RW: The extended home visit in psychiatric research and treatment. Psychiatry 26:168–175, 1963

16. Nielson J: Home visits by psychiatrists. Compr Psychiat 4:442–461, 1963

17. Speck R: Family therapy in the home. J Marriage Fam 26:72–76, 1964

Learning, Space, and Action in Family Therapy: A Primer of Sculpture

Frederick J. Duhl, M.D., David Kantor, Ph.D., and Bunny S. Duhl, B.A.

PREFACE

In which the authors orient the reader to their framework or concepts

IT would be a mistake for the reader to approach this paper with the belief that "family therapy" is another therapeutic technique to add to the psychiatric armamentarium. Instead, it is important to consider that "family therapy" is the easiest and least threatening rubric under which to present an essentially different approach for understanding and intervening in human behavior. This paper is truly not about family therapy. It is about *systems* and how to intervene in them, thereby changing individual behavior.

First, stop to re-think the very concept of therapy. The term "therapy" as used in psychiatry is a misnomer, since we do not cure. Psychosocial interventions, be they individual psychoanalysis or group therapy, provide opportunities for learning. That is, we therapist-teachers influence the minds of those we "treat" by offering opportunities to take in new information, or to reorganize the framework through which information is perceived and stored. We have also developed ways to improve the accessibility to consciousness of previously stored as well as new information and to foster the development of new logics and problem-solving methods. The total process is more properly called *learning*, not cure. As therapist-teachers who actively facilitate such learning, we must come to understand how individuals learn. Such awareness includes not only a process internal to that individual, but the processes of the systems in which the individual lives and learns. The first system is the family. Only after some time do school, community, or work systems become immediately relevant.

LEARNING

In which the authors describe how they think people take in information, process it, and act, thereby learning

In this paper we intend to look at some methods we have used to facilitate learning in individuals and families. The particular ones we have chosen are active and physical. This is not by happenstance.

The original processes by which the individual takes in information, organizes it, stores it, and acts upon it, are determined genetically by the brain structure available at birth. The physiology of the brain at birth has already been influenced by prenatal or constitutional factors that may delay maturational development (retardation) or selectively limit particular learning (as in

---

Reprint requests should be addressed to Frederick J. Duhl, M.D., 55 Williston Road, Brookline, Mass. 02146.

© 1973 by Grune & Stratton, Inc.

minimal "brain damage" or learning disability), or provide for special abilities (as in musical or mathematical talent). There is enough evidence that, through behavioral training, brain processes can be influenced through psychosocial processes over time. In general, however, we would see the learning style as a given that does not change markedly over time.

In understanding how people learn we look at the intake, organizing, and output modes as those which influence the understanding of all information that comes from internal or external sources.

Basic building blocks of learning such as perceptual capacities, visual-motor coordination, sequencing, and time conceptualization, are critical not only in formal "school learning" but in the learning about self and other, relationships, affective expression and control, communication, and the fulfillment of psychologic as well as physical needs and wants.

In our understanding, the child *learns to learn* also through the organizing messages from the people around him, or her, from birth. Verbal and nonverbal messages from members of the family system of which the individual is a part are influential in developing the individual's primary epistemologic position. Unless the individual can take in new information, he cannot change and cope with change.

If, in the course of the child's development, parents are not tuned into, or do not respect the child's particular style of learning, then the messages given by the parent may not be the messages received by the child. It would be similar to expecting a child to grow on a milk diet, when he happened to be allergic to milk. The "fit" of food offered to food retained is the issue, not whether the food is good or the child a bad eater. Many family systems problems can be reduced conceptually to a poor information or communication "fit," which leads to the following sequence: (1) poor information exchange; (2) lack of shared meanings; (3) inability of the child to map or learn new information; (4) inability of the child to cope as expected; (5) negative rewards for the child who is seen as a "failure"; (6) negative rewards for the parent who may feel guilty or a "failure" as parent; (7) reinforcement of the whole process through cycling; (8) ritualized coping techniques and inflexibility of learning; and (9) "symptoms" and low self-esteem for the child.

On the other hand, processes of learning with a good fit are as follows:

(1) Good information exchange with validation of child's perceptions and meanings;

(2) Shared meanings between parent and child;

(3) New information taken in and organized by child with parents' facilitation;

(4) New coping actions and options open to child;

(5) Child rewarded for coping response;

(6) Parent rewarded for "parenting";

(7) Learning of new coping techniques and learning how to learn increased;

(8) High self-esteem for child and parent.

Therapy as Learning

In which the authors state their beliefs as well as their values

The process of therapy is one of learning. Given the sequences we have outlined above, one can see that therapy often consists of learning things the individual could easily have learned at an earlier time, but for the unique family system processes of which he or she was a part. At times therapy is learning things that could *not* have been learned easily, because the individual's cognitive development was out of phase with the system at the time messages were sent. At times, it is the unlearning of patterns and processes that are no longer functional.

Even before a therapist outlines his techniques for learning, he or she should try to be open about his or her values. We would state ours as follows:

(1) We respect the *uniqueness* as well as the commonality of the individual.

(2) We believe the individual must have *optimal control* of his or her own destiny and personal space as long as he or she does not cause harm to others.

(3) We believe that people living within human systems must be *open* so as to influence, as well as be influenced, in order to survive in a changing society.

(4) We believe individuals as well as systems live developmentally over time, *tending toward differentiation, complexity and integration.*

(5) We believe humans are unique in their ability to give *meaning to experience,* to utilize cognitive processes to prepare for behavior, and to communicate verbally through the abstraction of language as well as physically or nonverbally.

(6) We believe that the individual can change only if he/she can *transcend* the system which is his/her context, and he/she cannot transcend it until he/she knows how it works.

SYSTEMS

In which the authors begin to define how hard it is to learn about systems

We, thus far, have outlined our concepts of individuals learning and developing within a system. We have stated the values we have that delimit our therapeutic teaching. Systems are complex in that so much happens simultaneously. Not every brain is organized to conceptualize multiple simultaneous activities, not to take in information from several sources at once and integrate it. However, in order to transcend a system, one must know it. In large measure, the action techniques we use are meant to help people know the systems of which they are a part, and thus change their roles in them.

Our approach to this type of action learning, sculpture, has been derived by David Kantor, through focusing on the common aspect of systems: space, time, and energy. These aspects are parameters of systems that all children must conceptualize (see Piaget).

Let us first reconsider space.

The Concept of Space

In which the authors describe something that is taken for granted

Think, if you will, about space. Not just the emptiness of the galaxy in which planets, stars, and moons exist in a patterned arrangement, but the immediate space in which all systems, especially living ones, are located. As a basic dimension of all systems, it is one that is taken for granted, as is the air we breathe. This neutrality to our perception is only questioned when we experience it anew through (1) a change in our processes of perception; (2) a change in the number and/or relationships of persons or objects in the space; or (3) a threat to, or invasion of, the boundaries of the space itself by others. Under these conditions, the space, which is usually ground in the figure-ground relationship, is experienced as the figure and, therefore is describable.

It should be noted that space is not seen as emptiness, once the boundary or edge of someone or something solid defines it. Sculptors like Henry Moore have spoken of and used the air surrounded by stone or bronze as another medium to be shaped. The shape of the space in which we live can be presented if we can only find a way to define the outlines of that shape. Sometimes "empty" space is perceived as the extension of the person or an object that it surrounds.

Consider the instruction to allow one car length between your car and the one in front of you for every 10 mph of speed on the highway. The car lengths define a measure of space that is as much a part of the car as the front bumper. Although it has no physical solidity, the defined space is functionally an extension of the car and the driver. Should it be entered, there is a good chance that contact with the solid car would be made and more concrete consequences follow. Similarly, the concept of "personal space" that surrounds an individual (which has been well stated by Edward Hall*) presumes an invisible boundary that is only recognized by the consequences of its being entered. We would extend that so as to state that *all systems not only inhabit space but are surrounded by a functional space and an invisible though meaningful boundary.*

Spatial Representations of a System

In which the authors consider how to present in words the "indescribable" space that a system inhabits as well as the relationships of the parts of the system

Let us consider then, the family system, its space, and the personal spaces within the system that surround and are inhabited by individuals. If the system at a given moment in time were sculpted by a Henry Moore (as he has done), then the spatial relations between the members could be statically represented, i.e., sculpted. However, family systems are alive and constantly changing; they expand and contract in the number of members. Children come and go as do parents and others. Indeed, even the sizes and shapes of the individuals change in time.

Considering only the number of members, the space to contain them, and the balancing and negotiating of personal space, a sculpture would have to be in constant flux over a single generation of a family life cycle. An observer of such a moving sculpture would need to observe from another rate of time. If we could speed up the sculpture as is done in a stop-action movie of the unfolding of a flower, then we could get the full sense of the overall rhythmic

---

*Edward T. Hall, author of *The Hidden Dimension.*

cycle. How might Henry Moore sculpt the dimensions of the multidimensional family?

The large global changes over the long reaches of family history, the births, deaths, separations, can be represented by changes in the mass of the sculpture. However, there are also aspects of family relationships over smaller segments of time, such as fighting and loving, intimacy and independence, and loss and replacement, which can be represented by distance and closeness in space. The dimensions of power and status can also be located in three-dimensional space.

Finally, to add to the complexity of the spatial representation of the system, we would ask our sculptor to consider the movements of the family members in relation to each other. Speed, randomness and regularity, intensity, and rhythm are all qualities of motion that can be abstracted and represented in a moving sculpture.

We can see that a system, defined as a set of units (family members) having common properties, with relationships between them over time, is difficult to describe in written words. Yet, we experience it in all its simultaneous action daily. How difficult it is to understand a hockey game described over radio in linear words and sentences; how often we tend to simplify the action by describing only the actions of the player with the puck. But, the fact is that 12 people plus the three referees are in action at once on the ice, in motion, in and out of the playing space continuously. In family life, too, the action never ceases for each member, although one or another may be highlighted at any moment. And in families there is not even time out for commercials.

Action Techniques and Therapy

In which the authors discuss the problems of learning through action

Psychotherapy has a long history of being a "talking process" since Freud first was able to have people reveal their inner world through free associations in speech. It is in part because of Freud's influence that our society is more free to talk publicly about that which was previously kept private.

Psychoanalysis and psychodynamic psychotherapy place associations to internally generated words, body experiences, and images as central to their technique. Associations to external sensations during the therapy hour are limited, since external stimuli are consciously minimized by the therapist and the setting he provides. In a more active therapy, the sights, sounds, words, smells, movements, and presence of others evoke, simultaneously, associations, meanings, and behavior, in context. A broader, total retrieval of memories of the individual within his erstwhile system is possible.

Learning and relearning through action techniques, therefore, is system-oriented.

At the same time, we are more and more convinced that inner psychologic adaptation without change in social behavior is not sufficient outcome for therapy. The old joke that, after psychoanalysis, a Van Gogh who would still cut off his ear, but would know why, is, as Freud points out, the revelation of truth in humor. The marriage fails; the patient has insight, but his behavioral contribution to the failure does not change. It is important that changes in behavior become the outcome criteria of therapy, not just inner understanding.

Thus, learning is conceptualized as having an end point in new behavior, not just in understanding.

Action approaches to therapy have a 50-yr history since Ferenczi and Wilhelm Reich. Today's therapeutic field is crammed with action. Again, the outcome must be judged not in the therapy sessions, but within the context of the family's daily life.

Thus, we must differentiate behavior encouraged in therapy to produce learning from those behaviors in the family or social setting that indicate real change. If the daily family context is also present in the erstwhile privacy of therapy, it will be easier for the continuity of learning. Nevertheless, there is no guarantee that learning within the therapeutic milieu will continue in the family's world. For some families, the therapeutic system and space act as a buffer and the therapist as a go-between that facilitates the development of new information and communication. The therapeutic task is to provide learning that will be generalized to spaces other than the one the therapist controls.

If at least one member of a family system carries out of the therapy a changed awareness and is free to act upon it, learning can continue in the family space.

We have previously indicated that only through awareness of the family system and the ability to transcend it through action that change in the family system will take place.

Let us now look at an action technique invented by David Kantor and developed at the Boston Family Institute and the Boston State Hospital Family Training Program over the past 4 yr.

SCULPTURE

In which the authors finally begin the description of technique

Sculpture is a dynamic, active, nonlinear process that portrays relationships in space and time so that events or attitudes may be perceived and experienced simultaneously. It is meant to provide the meanings, metaphors, and images of relationships in a way that can be shared by all who participate and observe. Information is not talked about but experienced through action and observation. An opportunity is provided for the presentation of a map rather than word description. It restates in action patterns behavior that language has used as metaphor. "I can't get close to him." "He turned his back on me." "I've felt distant since he said that." All these are colorful phrases into which sculpture breathes life again.

We, too, often forget that the children we once were lived in a nonverbal world in which spatial perceptions and affect were intimately connected. We have renounced the physical aspects of our early learning, although we still respond to them unconsciously. Making this dimension of learning live again intensifies the experience. Sculpture thus can be used in all arenas of learning about people.

In this paper, we have chosen to describe three variations of sculpture that we have developed, categorized by the number of people involved at any one moment. These are: (1) individual, (2) boundary or dyadic, (3) family or group.

Despite this categorization, all share the same aspects: the revelation of personal perceptions mediated by cognitive processes translated into behavior in context and over time. In each, at the very least, the revelation of his own perceptions and meanings is observed by himself, and the monitor or therapist. In dyadic or family sculpture, the differentiation of perceptions and meanings of two or more people is added as a goal in order to clarify the assumptions on which those other members of the same system have been acting.

The roles include: (1) *the sculptor,* who risks to reveal his private view; (2) *the monitor,* or therapist who guides the sculptor toward clarity and definition; (3) *the actors,* who lend themselves to portray members of the sculptor's system *only* as the sculptor sees them; and (4) *the audience,* who observes and comments from its special vantage point as observer to the whole process.

If the monitor and sculptor are present alone, then the other roles may be taken by them, or inanimate objects such as chairs. If video is available, observation and feedback of the total process including the audience's actions is also possible.

In order to preserve the *sculptor's* freedom to risk his revelations, the *monitor* protects the process. He sets the tone so that the sculptor's work does not become a performance for the audience's amusement. He guides the sculptor through questions and comments, following clues and communications with therapeutic sensitivity but without imposing his own perceptions. The *process of sculpture* is his to own and share, but not the content. The monitor is responsible for the pacing, timing, and flow of the process, guiding the players in their parts as described by the sculptor. He may evoke through his own words, tones, and actions, the memories, feelings and concepts of the sculptor. It is the monitor's responsibility to decide when to push into the "grey" or unclear areas and when to call a halt. His control, like a therapist's, is present and protective, but in the service of the sculptor's own uniqueness.

The sculpture begins by having the monitor and sculptor stand. The monitor helps the sculptor establish the particular situation, event of meaning, or family process he wishes to explore. Then, the monitor pushes for a point in time that would best fit the search. Evoking the scene, he asks the sculptor to close his eyes and imagine himself "there"—then he asks for a description of the image.

First the sculptor is asked to pace out the family space on the floor, delineating its size and shape. It is important that the sense of the space be described not only as the reality, "a large house" or "a railroad flat," but as metaphoric space.

The coloring and atmosphere of the space, its light and darkness, its warmth, the texture of its floor and surfaces, and the quality of its boundaries, are all evoked by questions. "Are you walking on eggshells?" "Are there windows or solid walls?" "How do you or others get in and out?" It is very much like establishing a stage setting which is not realistic but captures a mood.

The monitor is calling into play the kinesic and sensory associations of the sculptor. As the associations return, the sculptor may seem to enter a new state of consciousness as revealed by glassy eyes and bodily revelations of affect. Not every sculptor enters that state, but many do. In this, the monitor's therapeutic talent and sense of timing play a large part. As the stage is set, the monitor may describe the total setting back to the sculptor, allowing for corrections. Once the setting is felt to be complete, the monitor brings on the *players,* by asking the sculptor to people his family space with family members and other significant people, one by one. The sculptor chooses other members of the training group, or the real family, to portray the family members not present, as in the family of origin of the sculptor. In what seems a magical way, sculptors in training seminars often choose people whose qualities and experiences are similar to the characters to be portrayed.

Placing the Players in Space

In which a fictitious person called Joan sculpts a family

Let us try to describe the process of placing the players in the family space with an example. Joan was sculpting her family when she was age six, having picked a time when her father was out of work. The space had been described as "light in the kitchen with a dark other room" where Father was alone listening to the radio.

The first person of choice, which has its own significance, was her father. She looked around the training group and selected Bob, whose solemnity she felt reminded her of him. She was asked to tell Bob what he needed to know to play her father, and Bob was instructed to ask questions of her as if he were the father.

"Am I a quiet man?"

"Yes, very depressed."

"Do I seem busy? How do I move?"

"You're quiet and speak to no one until they come to you."

The monitor asked that Joan give Bob a typical gesture that summarized her father for her. She suggested he sit down and hold his head in his hands with his body turned away into the corner. As Bob tried this, he checked with Joan as to whether he had done it right.

The monitor kept the dialogue succinct, so that Joan did not talk *about* Father but *to* him, using the present tense. She was instructed to place father in the family space, which she did and to position herself in relation to him with a characteristic pose. In this situation the pose could not be static, for Joan moved in towards Father and out again. Bob asked if his own gestures or pose changed with her movement. In this case it did not.

Once Father was set in position, Joan was asked to select someone else. She chose Grace to play Mother, saying Grace's smile reminded her of her parent. Grace was also the oldest woman in the group and as such was often chosen as Mother. After giving Grace the busy movements of Mother, Joan was encouraged not only to place her in relation to both herself and Father but she was then asked to suggest patterns of movement to both Mother and Father. With the addition of Mother, the sense of a system developed.

By this time Joan understood the process of sculpting and, without too much aid from the monitor, added Doug as her young brother, age 2, and Lynn as her sister, age 4, giving them positions and gestures, appropriate to their ages. As the sculpture developed, it appeared that only her 4-yr-old sister moved in and out of Father's dark space freely. The sculpture was alive. "Was anyone else in the home?", the monitor asked. "Oh, yes," recalled Joan, "my Uncle Jack; he lived with us until I was ten. He was not really my uncle; he was a boarder." Placing her "uncle" in the family sculpture, she put him next to Mother, giving Bill, who played "Uncle" Jack, gestures of warmth and openness.

With the players in place, the monitor encouraged them to move and act, *without words,* in the patterns given them. In moments, an overall systemic pattern emerged. Joan was now totally immersed in the associative memory of the past. More and more affect began to show as she took in the stimuli of her own actions and others. The overall pattern was ritualized through the monitor's command to repeat it over and over. The ritualization locked the players into the feelings the players were experiencing. Suddenly Joan stopped. "God, I don't want to go into Father's room!...It's not that *he* kept me out. *I* don't want to go in. I want to be with Jack and Mother."

By this time, Bill and Grace, caught up in the patterns, had moved closer to each other, revealing in action an intimacy not hinted at before. Joan had observed it, as had the monitor. To the monitor it was clear there was a "gray space," a family secret, emerging.

The monitor suggested that Mother and Jack move closer. Suddenly, Joan blurted out: "Don't do that!" as if she were again 6 yr old. She regained her composure — "I used to wonder about that," she said.

As memories were recalled and placed into the system context of the sculpture, Joan questioned the possibility of an affair between Mother and "Uncle" Jack during the time father was depressed.

More information could have been revealed by questioning Joan, but the monitor, feeling that enough of immediate significance had been revealed, stopped the unfolding of the sculpture and began another phase. Although the actors and the audience, their curiosity heightened, wanted to squeeze more from Joan, the monitor took control to protect her from being overloaded or used by the group for their voyeuristic needs.

The Feedback Stage

While continuing the example, the authors describe a process in which an important dimension of information is made available, and the sculptor is moved from the narcissistic belief that he is central to the family system

The monitor, by bringing down the curtain on this first scene, began not only to provide some space for Joan to return from her memories, but also to take on an observing role. It must be noted here that it is not always easy for the sculptor to return. The transition process must be sensitively facilitated by the monitor. At the same time, the sculptor is asked by the monitor, who now acts like a modern Copernicus, to decentrate*, to cease from viewing the family system as revolving around himself.

---

*To give up the egocentric view of an event and replace it by milticentric views of the event. It is part of the process by which a system is known from many vantage points so that it may be understood in its complexity and thus transcended.

In our example, Joan was asked to listen to the feedback of the actors. In turn, the actors were asked to verbalize how it felt to be in the role and space that Joan had allocated to them.

Bill told how lonely he felt as Father since no one except Lynn came into his room. He also wondered what was going on in the rest of the family, but felt helpless to act. To interact with anyone or come out of his room was an ordeal.

Joan confirmed that Father hated to go out on family walks as the rest did on Sundays. Grace, as Mother, said that she felt she had lost Father; it was like a living death. She needed someone to comfort her with three young children demanding her attention. She was angry at Father and was glad Jack was living there. "Uncle" Jack said he felt more and more like a father to the kids and liked it. He felt upset about Father but was hesitant to visit his private space due to guilt.

"That's right," said Joan, "you really stayed away from Dad."

Bill spoke up. "Did you realize you put your hand up as you walked toward me? You didn't want to see me either. That hurt."

"I did?" asked Joan.

The group and the monitor confirmed it.

"You're right! I didn't want to go to him. I didn't like that darkness and him sitting with the radio all the time. It was spooky! And, I always thought I wanted to be with him!"

The players' responses had begun to bring new information also, as they indicated to Joan what others in the family system might have been feeling or experiencing, although this had never been communicated or shared previously in the original family.

The multi-centric aspects of a family system in which all the members have their own perceptions and meanings becomes apparent at this stage of the process of sculpture. It is the goal of any system intervention to facilitate the active understanding of this multi-centricity so that different viewpoints may be appreciated and validated, and may influence behavior.

To facilitate this understanding, the audience is encouraged to provide observations of the total process. These tend to reveal the system as a whole. At the same time, the audience feeds back the observed nonverbal behavior of all the players, including the sculptor, and checks out the inner experiences revealed by the actions.

As the total group gets caught up in the processing of the information they have observed together, the monitor begins a search for the metaphor that captures the essence of the family system. Sometimes this is easily derived, such as "the family was like a cage of tigers, with everyone pacing and alone." The arrival of a metaphor captures and stamps the total experience in a creative poetic image.

In the fictional example we have presented, the sculptor set out to understand the experience of her family at a critical point in time and found a family secret. Other sculptures focus on special dimensions of family systems such as power or intimacy, placing relationships between two or more family members in a larger context. Some may make explicit the larger networks in which the family system is imbedded. Others delineate the family system over generations.

The topics are infinite, but we would like to present two other special uses of sculpture at this point.

DYADIC OR BOUNDARY SCULPTURE*

In which the authors describe how to clarify a two-person system, with both persons present, often in conflict

In dyads, such as couples, co-therapists, co-leaders, or co-students, issues of closeness and distancing, availability and shutting out, and poor "reading" of the other emerge as basic to a conflict. In these circumstances, we have found boundary sculpture an invaluable tool. Instead of allowing each individual to justify their own difficulty in understanding the other, boundary sculpture places the *responsibility for awareness* of each person squarely on the shoulders of the other.

All systems have an ordering to them which may be formulated as "laws" or "rules." Members of a family will act under the influence of certain rules of behavior, whether these rules have been verbalized or not. These rules will often define what behavior is acceptable, in what context and with whom. If family rules are not clear and accepted by all, members may run into conflict, they invade one another in some dimension. When rules are verbalized they may be changed to fit the present realities of the system. One way of clarifying the conflicting rules that lie behind conflicting behaviors and invasions between any two or more people is the use of boundary sculpture.

In describing this process, we need to state that it makes no difference whether the two persons concerned are family members, co-therapists, or people on a job. What will be brought to the foreground by boundary sculpture is that one person's rules governing his space were only *assumed* to be known by the other person, or were completely unknown, so that the behavior of one was judged in the context of the rules of the other.

In a boundary sculpture, the monitor or therapist will ask one person to walk around the room and feel out his personal space, that space which he always carries with him, in which his sense of self lives. Once the sculptor has described that space, the monitor sums it up in words and asks if he has understood correctly. This validates the sculptor who is given a chance to correct himself. The monitor then asks him how he, the sculptor, gets out of or leaves *his space*. By asking this, the monitor can further determine how much the sculptor is in charge of his own space. The control of one's own space is vital to one's self-esteem. If one does not control his own space, he is at the mercy of others, and his self-esteem is in others' hands.

The second step is to ask the sculptor to describe who can enter and under what conditions it would be possible. To help him in this differentiating process, the monitor can use himself, or others in the room, including, if necessary, the other person in the dyad as the person making entry. It usually works better if in this process, the "other person" is audience and observer to the first sculptor's description and processes. The monitor sequentially asks how the sculptor would act instinctively and without words to the entry of a male or

---

*Originated by Bunny S. Duhl and Jeremy Cobb, M.A., at the Boston State Hospital.

female stranger, acquaintance, and intimate. One person, at a time, appropriate to the defined role, tries to enter the sculptor's space without words as the sculptor reacts.

Several things occur during this part of the boundary sculpture. In action and reaction, the sculptor will be defining the rules and conditions that another must follow in order to be allowed into his personal space. Issues of energy and impact will be raised, especially if the "actors" playing roles in the sculpture vary the speed, intensity, and direction by which they enter. If one purposely ignores the "door in front" and tries to break through the "rear wall," then the variety of rules and meanings come to light. The sculptor further will be differentiating his uniqueness, in the manifestations of the control of personal space. The monitor aids in this differentiation by providing the sculptor with information as to the differences in his responses to male and female acquaintances, strangers, and intimates. It is important that the monitor be creative in his questioning and choices of actors' roles, zeroing in on those that help in any differentiating process. In our presentation, we can only offer guidelines of areas to be explored, for boundary sculptures are as varied as the people monitoring and sculpting them.

One can ask and enact, if there are several observers, what happens when the sculptor has multiple "invasions" at one time. Most often it is preferable to assign a role or roles, and then do it, without too many words, so that the sculptor's actions are "fresh" and not prepared through thought.

Information is given to the sculptor all along the way, not only in terms of what he, sculptor, did or looked like, but also how the actor perceived and experienced him. "I feel I could walk right through you, even though you said your boundary was way out here. You did nothing to stop me."

Statements such as these underline for the sculptor how unclear his messages are, how incongruent his thoughts and behaviors are, and how *he* is responsible for his own actions for defining and protecting or not protecting his own boundaries. Often, the way the boundary is defined has a history to it, based on the sculptor's early sensory capacity. Poor eyesight often makes for close boundaries.

The monitor can then ask how the sculptor brings others *into* his space. One way of highlighting this process is to ask, "How do you get someone into your own space without words?" (acquaintance, friend, intimate, male, female, mother, brother, etc.). During the mime, the other actor can be uninvolved, mildly involved, or intensely involved in doing "his own thing" when the sculptor approaches for engagement.

What is revealed here is the richness or poverty of the sculptor's "bag of tricks" to bring someone he wants into his space. A myriad of actions are possible, but the ones chosen by the sculptor further delineate his sense of self in coping with others. Is he creative or rigid in his approach? Does he try alternates if one approach does not get the person to join him? Does he use force? Eye contact? Any seductive procedures? Does he "hang in" doggedly? Does he smile? And, so on. Each of these reveal another aspect of himself.

Again, the actor(s) feeds back to the sculptor: "I finally went with you because I couldn't resist anymore, you'd tried so many ways." The sculptor again finds some new information on how his behavior affects another.

One can ask the "other person" to enter the sculptor's space, without words, as he usually does. If there has been a problem between these two people, we may guess the entrance has been perceived as an invasion in some dimension by the sculptor, who will react in an "invaded" manner. The monitor can then ask the other person to enter again, with the information he now has about the sculptor's boundaries and how the sculptor would like people to enter.

Based on our experience, the sculptor, whose boundaries are now understood, will react in an accepting manner and will allow for the other's newly learned style of entry. This same total process is then repeated with the other half of the dyad. The original sculptor becomes audience.

At the end of this second defining process, the monitor can ask each person in the dyad, one at a time, to now "go get the other person" and bring him into his space, first, as is usually done and, second, in the way that he now knows the other wants. There is continual feedback from the other person in each encounter. The monitor then suggests a paradoxic confrontation to underscore the nonrewarding behavior. He insists that each partner approach the other in the "old" manner several times, as if new information did not exist.

Once these boundaries and the processes by which they are crossed are defined in action, each person can no longer act as if the other's rules of behavior were the same as one's own. If one continues to act in the old way with "negative" results, he is solely responsible. One is free to act any way he wishes, but the blame game can no longer be played. Ignorance of the other can no longer be claimed. New information now can be translated into new options for behavior. The monitor can reinforce this new "understanding," asking the dyad to interact together, in a new way, then and there. He gives them a mutual issue to deal with or problem to solve in space, without words. If two people have an ongoing relationship, and any motivation for a "smoother" one exists, they will then have new options to try.

The pathway to new information about self and other has thus been opened in a shared way, with *feedback* and *without put-down* for each person's uniquenesses and perceptions. Each half of the dyad is free to explore his own and each other's meanings in a new way. They are free to experiment within the new shared "rules of behavior" and even free to change the rules. For, as one finds one's boundaries accepted and not invaded, one tends not to need those boundaries with that other person in quite the same way. People struggle to maintain their sense of self, their "territory," their intactness, against invasion from outside. If another person respects, validates, and acts within the rules of those boundaries, the need to protect them from that person's invasion drops away and, thus, the rules, or boundaries, can change, and the conflicts cease to exist.

FAMILY SCULPTURE

*In which we work with an existing family or system
using a fictional example*

In boundary or dyadic sculpture the process is used to clarify the rules governing each part of a two-part system to the other. With family or group sculpture, the process helps define a larger and more complicated system.

In learning with and from a family about its system, sculpture can be used to particularize and highlight selected aspects of the system as it exists in the present. If, as therapists, we find that different members of the family are operating on different "rules" or assumptions of rules, we use sculpture to take the conflict out of the verbal mode, where it has been locked and unresolved, into the actional mode, thus allowing the entire family *and* the therapist to clearly experience each individual's meanings, in sequence within a short time.

Let us consider a fictional family in which Mother states, "We are a close family; I don't love one more than another. I treat each one equally." Such a statement is a combination of her perceptions and her internal rules, which define the ways a mother should act and feel. A mother must not show favoritism, since it may lead to conflict among siblings, and it is important for families to be close. If her rules are not shared, or her actions are not perceived by others as she perceives them, there will be conflict. Statements that are so total deserve to be checked out with all the members of the family.

The monitor-therapist, instead of relying on verbal affirmations or disagreements with Mother, transcends the possible immediate battle by developing a family sculpture along the dimensions of intimacy and closeness. Asking the family to think of the spaces between people as representative of emotional closeness, the therapist asks one family member to be sculptor and to position the other members in space, in relation to himself, and each other.

For many people, this process forces them for the first time to think through and "see" the quality of relationships they have taken for granted. It provides one setting in which the multiple perceptions and meanings in the family become available to all. Sharing the new task, they share their own version of the family system and the varied roles they play in it.

As Johnny places Mother 6 ft from himself, he makes a clear statement to her of their relationship from *his* point of view. The action is less risky than the verbal statement he has never dared to put into words. The monitor controls the possible negation of it by restating that it is John's perception, which *can* be different. As Johnny places Father right next to himself, the therapist asks "Are Mother and Father emotionally that far apart also?" John is thereby called upon to rethink two-person relationships as system relationships. His egocentric view of his hub-like position in the family and everyone's distance from him, is challenged by the need to fit *all* the parts together at once. "How do you see them not only in relation to yourself, but to each other?" he is asked. As John quickly resorts his perceptions and now adds other members to his sculpture, he finds it hard to avoid presenting it as a system.

In positioning people, John finds that distance alone does not describe the connections between them. The therapist helps him differentiate *and* organize his concepts by asking, "How does Mother touch Father? Does Mother need three arms to be close to the kids? Is Father always facing in toward Mother? Does Susan only reach Father through Mother? Do you mean her head has to swivel around like an owl's to be in touch with everyone? That must be a pain in the neck!"

John's vignette may take about 5–10 min to sculpt. As various members interrupt and claim, "That's not how it is, I'm not at all this close to Susan," the therapist protects John's power as the sculptor of the moment, freezes the family in their positions and reminds them that each member will have a turn to position the family as he or she experiences it. Again, the therapist is underscoring the concept of multiple truths, multiple perceptions and multiple realities, in every family. John may well have been permitted to complete his statement for the first time.

When John finishes his version of intimacy in his family, the therapist asks each member to make a mental note of how John sees himself and them in relation to each other. Then Susan, or Mother, or Father in turn becomes the sculptor and puts each family member in space in the same dimensions of emotional closeness and distance. Each family member thus reveals his own, and experiences each other's view of the family. Discrepancies, long shrouded by unchecked assumptions, become revealed. In the context of multiple views of a system, blame is harder to come by. Each member can define that his own feeling can be and is different. How he feels and how someone else might *want* him to feel or thinks he feels are two different levels of operation and meaning, which the therapist differentiates.

Intimacy is not the only area that can be explored. The therapist or the family might choose to depict power relationships in the family. Who makes decisions and who carries them out? Who can command and who must listen? Again, how does each member perceive himself in relation to others in their cross relationships?

One might find that there are contexts or conditions under which intimacy or power relationships change. For instance, "If Susan is around, I cannot be close to Father. When she isn't around, I can be very close to him. If Dad has had a bad day at the office, there is no reasoning with him. His word is law, and I would position him on a chair with a raised, clenched fist. However, if he's had a good day, I would position him here standing on the floor with me, with one arm and hand outstretched toward me."

People are most often unaware of their impact on the total family system and on each individual member in it. The information-giving and feedback process, which this type of sculpture embodies, allows this new information to be shared by all. The meaning that this new information has for each member of the family may well be different. But, again, unless one knows the system from a multicentric view, one cannot change it or transcend it.

OPTIONS AND FANTASIES IN FAMILY SCULPTURE

In which the therapist plays the game of "What if?" to induce new learning

When families are stuck in behaviors that are nonrewarding and nonadaptive for *their* collective or individual goals, those families are behaving *as if* (1) there were no options, or (2) any known options are unacceptable.

If the family and/or therapist finds that the second condition is operating, the therapist can ask each family member to sculpt how he would like it to be in the dimension to be explored. He gives sanction to fantasies, wishes, and dreams. After all, it is between the reality of what is and what one wishes that all changing behavior, all strivings, struggles, and growth take place.

Most often, if a family is stuck, they will have a difficult time revealing their wishes. What is experienced by the therapist as their "poverty of imagination" may also be the response to an unstated family rule, "Wishes are not allowed."

The therapist can use his position and power, to gently but firmly and even seductively state the alternative: Wishes *are* allowed. They exist in us all, even if we don't want them there or don't want to acknowledge them.

If the therapist can succeed in having the family share and make manifest their wishes about relationships, he has cracked open the door to options and to change.

Once this occurs, the family and therapist can explore the possible alternative behavior of family members. They are free then to dig deeper into the road-blocks, to change the myths and rules behind them. The therapist, in recognizing the uniqueness of each individual in his own context, can act as a bridge between generations, out of the material shared and revealed in the sculptures. He can suggest alternative behaviors for them to try right there in the sessions. Those that are found to be rewarding can be tried in daily life.

CREATIVE SCULPTURE

In which the authors speak directly to the reader so as to
provide some guidelines for the application of sculpture

Having read through our preface, with its framework for the approach, as well as some examples of sculpture, the reader may well be ready to try to use the technique in a therapeutic or learning situation. Therefore, some guidelines for using action techniques may be useful.

First of all, do not consider the ways of the authors to be the only ways. Consider that you, too, might be more creative than we are. But certainly do not avoid trying the approach as it has been outlined at least five times. By then you will have found out how to edit or improve it.

Second, do not consider that what has been presented is the full extent of the technique. The authors, and others at the Boston Family Institute, have been using sculpture since 1969, and have not yet begun to scratch the surface. So do not falsely believe that what you try on one occasion covers or represents the full spectrum of what can be done.

Third, let us suggest how to go about approaching any learning situation with sculpture.

When faced with a conflict or bind in the learning process, or between two or more members of a family group, first clarify the question, bind, conflict, or "resistance" in your own mind. Then "spatialize" it; that is, visualize it in your mind's eye as a spatial representation. Next, stop all talk except your own and get up out of your chair. Suggest that those in the bind take a risk and try something in action without words.

Set the stage through asking them to feel out and walk around the space; then suggest the action that will help them represent the process. Sometimes you may help the process by using yourself, a co-therapist, or one of the family or group members. Or, you may use chairs, coat racks, lamps, or animals. Or, you may be the monitor and comment and question as you go.

The use of actions without words should be followed by the debriefing, in which questions are asked about associations, perceptions, or observations, stimulated by the action.

Following the debriefing, relate it back to the other experiences in the learning or therapy sessions and then to experiences outside the room and to their own histories. If more than one person is in the learning space, have them comment on their observations. You may try the same procedure several times with one person and/or with others.

Think "space" and "action" until it comes naturally, like a second language, or, more realistically, like a primary language regained. After all, action in space is the child's original way of learning. Lastly, enjoy your exploration. There are no rules for creativity.

Audio–Visual Techniques in Family Therapy

Ian Alger, M.D.

A FAMILY that comes for treatment is usually one that has reached an equilibrium only at the great expense of one of its members. The therapist's intervention is designed to relieve the pain and suffering of the family members by creating possibilities for change in the system so that the "problem" behavior of the "identified patient" will no longer be a necessary function in that system. This kind of effect may be achieved sometimes rather simply, but at other times it may require a major reorientation of the entire family to the development of quite different goals, and quite different attitudes toward each other and toward life.

Be it large or small, however, the effect is achieved from a cybernetic viewpoint by changing the feedback into the system, and all the varied methods of therapy have this in common. The use of videotape playback during a therapy session is a method of introducing system-specific feedback during the ongoing process so that immediate corrections and alterations can be made, and new resolutions for that particular system can be achieved. To elaborate the cybernetic model further, the videotape playback may introduce negative feedback into a system in danger of runaway from an overload of positive feedback. To illustrate this, consider a family in which the mother desperately wants her young son to excel. Whenever he is about to do something, she either coaches him or initiates the action for him, with the result that he hesitates increasingly. In response, the mother becomes more active in pushing. Eventually, if the pattern is not interrupted, the runaway system includes a frantic, over-possessive mother and an inhibited, withdrawn son. When such a scene is replayed on videotape, a new possibility is introduced for the mother to see that the actual effect of her "help" is to inhibit rather than encourage the very activity she desires from her son. Technically, positive feedback encourages a system to continue in its same direction, like a thermostat that has become stuck and continually calls for more heat, and results in a runaway situation. In the case of the thermostat, the boiler might eventually explode. Negative feedback, on the other hand, calls for a change in the direction of the system, and promotes the development of equilibrium and stability. It is evident from this that the skill in therapy is to introduce information feedback that will halt runaways, but not produce new runaways of its own, while at the same time promoting new effects that will dislodge a system from an equilibrium that is functionally stale and nonproductive for its members.

Another important aspect that should be considered is that, although the "family system" is initially the one that is under consideration, it immediately becomes a "therapy system" when the therapist(s) joins with the family members in a therapeutic endeavor. (The word "endeavor" rather than "session"

Reprint requests should be addressed to Ian Alger, M.D., New York Medical College, 500 E. 77 Street, New York, N.Y. 10021.

is used to make the point that a new system is created whether or not all the members of it are assembled in one place at one time, such as in a therapy session. In other words, family therapy is a conceptual approach rather than a concrete technique.) Because the therapist is now a part of this system, it is especially useful in videotaping that his behavior along with that of the family members be included.

From this brief introduction perhaps it can be seen how the method of videotape playback is ideally suited to the practice of family therapy. Although the reality of an inner experience both past and present for each member of the family is recognized, the crucial importance of the context and of system behavior, both verbal and nonverbal, is emphasized in family therapy. The videotaping technique allows the collection of hitherto unavailable objective data of these behaviors, and permits the immediate replay of this material so that it can be integrated into the ongoing process.

EQUIPMENT

Videotape is a relative newcomer. Long before its appearance, therapists had used and continue to use photographs,[6] movie films, and sound recordings.[8] Indeed, cassette audiotapes have now become so practical and inexpensive that most therapists have recorders and use them not only for auditing lectures, but also for recording therapy sessions. With the development of inexpensive videotape recorders, which are dependable and efficient, the advantages of capturing both the action and sound, and the immediate playback without processing, have made this audio–visual technique preferable for the clinician.

Much sophisticated equipment is available, and in larger settings its use has special advantages, some of which will be briefly described later in this article. For the most part, however, simple equipment is very adequate, and has the additional merit of economy both of money and of effort during the actual therapy sessions. In an aside, let me explain that I am concentrating here only on the therapeutic use of videotape. Video techniques are of great value in training therapists, and also have unique attributes for research, but those considerations will be left for discussion elsewhere.[4,5]

The following aspects are important in developing an adequate videotape facility: setting, including room size, decoration, furnishings, and lighting; the actual recording equipment, including microphones; and, finally, the issues of concealment and who will operate the equipment. In a clinic or private office, the room can generally be the one in which families are regularly seen. If a one-way mirror is installed, the camera can be placed behind this. This has some advantages in minimizing the distraction, and in modifying the situation less, and, for these reasons, it is valuable in research projects. For use in therapy, however, concealment is not necessary, and the openness may actually be an advantage in including the equipment as part of the total situation. When a cameraman is used, his presence in the room can be best dealt with by announcing at the start that he should be considered part of the session, and that any reactions about him should be revealed, and that he also can react to the situation. The new half-inch video recorders are portable, and operate with very little noise, so their presence in the room is not distracting, and even without remote control switching, the therapist can easily play back any portion of the tape he wishes without difficulty.

The new cameras also will function well in ordinary room light, so special illumination is not necessary, and again this adds no unnatural quality to the atmosphere of the session. Families often arrange themselves for therapy in a semi-circular position, and this is ideal for videotaping. If a cameraman is not used, the therapist can operate the camera from his own place, usually at one end of the seating arrangement. In this simple type of set-up, one TV monitor (23-in diagonal) is all that is required. During the session, the monitor can be left on so participants can see direct feedback of the session, or at times the monitor can be put on stand-by position, and the pictures can be taken by watching the action through a viewfinder in the camera itself. At times, a useful procedure is to have different members of the family take turns operating the camera. In this way, each of them develops a new perspective from the point of view of the camera, and most people find that even when they are no longer operating the camera they still retain this new observational capacity. In addition, it is often helpfully revealing to learn on which aspects of the family each member focuses. Some tend to avoid angry expressions, others focus on sexual aspects, while still others may exclude some member of the family altogether. This kind of data can be discussed usefully in the family session.

In summary, then, all that is required for a simple installation is a half-inch videotape deck, a TV monitor, and a camera and tripod. The camera can be equipped with a zoom lens, and this adds to the versatility by allowing for close-up shots, which at times are especially revealing of facial expressions and convey very sensitive bits of information. A regular, or wide-angle lens, on the other hand, gives a much better view of the interactions in the group, and catches easily the way the group may be fragmenting, and how members may be forming alliances. Finally, the question of recording the sound in the session is especially important. Often, good pictures are taken but the sound quality is neglected. Usually an omni-directional microphone placed near the floor in front of the semi-circle grouping will be adequate. At times, when better fidelity is needed, e.g., when a member of the family has a very quiet voice, lavaliere microphones may be used, although the presence of many cords tends to be disturbing, and also tends to discourage movement in the group.

In more complex studios, several cameras and monitors may be installed, with the use of a special-effects generator. This latter piece of equipment permits the mixing of signals from different cameras, with split-screen effects, and corner inserts, as well as superimposition of images. Certain special techniques can be utilized if this equipment is available, and in a later section a short description of some of these will be included. However, let it be stated once again that excellent results can be obtained with the basic system of one camera, one recorder, and one monitor, and that this can be readily operated as easily as a home television console, so even the mechanically less-skilled therapist will have no problem. In addition, the expense for such an outfit is now less than $2,000, and the reliability of the transistorized units is very high, so that repairs and maintenance are minimal.

APPLICATIONS

Videotape is a most versatile tool, and the variety of ways in which it can be used is limited only by the imagination and ingenuity of the therapists. A few of the more common methods will be outlined here. A family session may be recorded, and then played back in its entirety immediately following the session, or at a later time, possibly just before the next session. Another variation is to provide a viewing room in order that the family may look at the playback session at its convenience. With cassette recorders it is now possible to have the family take a recorder home so they can review the tape there between sessions. This latter technique has been most useful with audiotapes, even though these are definitely more difficult to follow than videotapes.

A second method is to record an arbitrary segment of a session, say 10 or 15 min, and then spend the remainder of the time in a playback review of that portion. This is an especially valuable way to introduce the technique because the random segment does not carry any special significance, and allows greater freedom for the family to become familiar in recognizing the kinds of information revealed on the tape.

A method of focused replay has been advocated by Stroller,[9] who felt that a much more significant impact could be achieved when the therapist selected segments that illustrated important interpersonal reactions, and group dynamics.

A variation of this same idea occurs when "ad-lib." use of specific replay is allowed during a session. In this method, the therapist, or any member of the family can interrupt at any time during the session and call for an instant replay of a particular section. This may involve the person himself, or any other member, or grouping of members. As with any of the replay methods, the fact that the same material can be played and replayed as many times as desired has the additional advantage of allowing people to focus first on one aspect of the segment, then on another. For example, a son may call attention to his father's stern look, and then on additional replay it may be noted that at the same time the mother was looking beseechingly towards the father, while still another replay may reveal the hitherto unnoticed fact that the father had tears in his eyes.

EFFECTS

The reactions to the videotape will vary depending on the phase of therapy. If it is suggested that making videotapes of the sessions may be a useful adjunct in the treatment, most families are agreeable. Assurance is given that the tapes will be used only in the actual treatment unless otherwise stated, and in the latter case for educational purposes with other professionals, and then only if written consent is given by the participants.

In viewing tapes for the first time, most people concentrate on their own image, and even though they may have seen themselves on home movies, the effect of the videotape has greater immediacy. The "image impact"[1] may be positive or negative overall, and then certain specific features may be identified, such as an "attractive smile," or more generally such as "a relaxed look." Regardless of the negative or positive reaction, experience clinically suggests that if the reaction to the image is strong there is a good likelihood that the person will find the videotape experience useful, whereas those with a more indistinct reaction may be affected little.

After the initial playback experience, more attention can be paid to the context and to the interactions among the family group. The tone for the whole family may be set by one facial expression or by a posture. For example, one mother's timid and frightened mien cast an atmosphere of tentativeness over her family, and all the members could be seen constantly checking out her reaction after each move. In another family, the son's diffident slouch enraged the father, while the son's curled lip to each statement from his mother brought a flush of anger to her face.

Such behavior is readily seen on the replay, although often, when it had been commented upon in the regular session, there has been a denial. A case in point is the son who exclaimed, "What do you mean disrespectful, I was *just* sitting here listening to you." True, he was listening, but even he nodded his head in understanding when he recognized his sneer on the replay. This faculty of defining the discrepancies between verbal and nonverbal channels of communication is one of the most useful attributes of the method. The sending of such double and discrepant messages, with the simultaneous denial of one of them is the basis for double-binding communication, and as Bateson et al.[3] have elaborated, can be the basis of severe symptomatic behavior. The playback allows confirmation that both messages did indeed exist, and, for this reason, it is not only reassuring to the person who reacted, but is also enlightening for the sender, who may for the first time become aware of the reasons why he is getting the kind of negative reactions that may have been puzzling to him.

Other discrepancies may occur between two nonverbal communications. For example, a husband may be listening to his wife with a smile indicating his accord, while at the same time he may be seated with his legs crossed against her while he is leaning away from her, indicating his disagreement and his desire to disassociate himself from her.

Clues as to who may be an initiator in a sequence can also be gained by noticing that certain movements by two people seem synchronous. On careful replay, one is often surprised to see that the apparently submissive family member is actually the one who first initiated the sequence, and is indeed the subtle choreographer. Other more clear-cut directional cues may be identified, such as the pointing of a finger indicating a response is required, the holding up of a palm to call a halt, and the sweeping hand gesture of dismissal, with a sideward toss of the head, and a downward glance of negation. Problematic behavior in some members becomes understood when seen in the context of the other messages being sent by gestures, postures, and the grouping itself.

Indeed, the way the family arranges itself is recognized to be of extreme significance, both as to the dynamic structure of the family transactions, and as to the possibilities for movement by the individual members. Changes in the alliances can be traced on the replay, and the formation of dyads and triads can easily be defined in relationship to the flow of the group process.

Subjective reactions, that is, feelings of the members of the family, can also be movingly identified on replay. A person who is completely unaware of a feeling may recognize a facial expression, and, from this, suddenly may develop a new understanding of his own reaction. For example, a young woman suddenly exclaimed as she looked at herself listening to her brother tell of his anxiety over a forthcoming examination, "Oh, I look so serious there, so pained . . . I now see I really was feeling for him, and yet I remember that all I was thinking was that it served him right to feel bad because he hadn't studied. But now I can also feel how sorry I am for you (turning to her brother)." Also occurring frequently is the reverse kind of situation, in which a person is aware of a feeling inside himself, but completely unaware that his expression is noncommunicative. One husband, after seeing the replay of his impassive face during his wife's tearful explanation of a situation, said, "My God, I was feeling so badly for you, and yet as I look at my face I can see that you would have no idea of that!" This has been called the "second chance phenomenon," because following the replay, a person has a second chance to express the feelings that originally were present, but which were unknowingly hidden during the actual incident.

As the videotape method is integrated increasingly into the therapy sessions, each member of the family is encouraged to utilize it, and to participate as an equal in making observations and in reporting reactions. In this process the therapist is included as well, and it is in this way that the videotape playback makes a most important contribution to the democratization of the therapeutic process. Often the therapist has been endowed with (and even has taken upon himself) special power to make significant observations and interpretations. By the very nature of such a hierarchical process, the therapist must of necessity become removed from the level of an equal participant, and elevated to the position of reporter-observer at best, and judge at worst. When objective data are provided by the tape, and everyone has an equal chance to comment, and to refer back to the "way it is," a more genuine research effort is encouraged, in which parents and children, spouse and therapist alike become coworkers in a common project. When the problem in many families asking for therapy is that one member is being scapegoated, the value of a method that can so readily take the focus off the identified patient and shift it to the total interactional context can readily be appreciated. The forcefulness with which the replay can demonstrate the family process is reflected in its therapeutic usefulness.

Lasting Effects

Clinical experience suggests that people are able to retain the visual portrayal of an awareness more vividly than a verbal conceptualization. A concrete visual image can have great impact, similar to the kind of synthesizing imagery some dreams provide. At any rate, patients years later may refer to a particularly striking image, such as, "I'll never forget that lost look I had. I decided then I was really going to look after myself." Or, "I never knew I was so pretty!" One husband saw himself mirroring every movement of his wife, and in that instant decided he was going to find his own direction and stop orienting his life entirely to his wife's actions.

Another lasting effect has been the capacity of family members to recognize double messages, and then comment upon them and continue to clarify the communicational levels, so that the frequency of crossed communication is diminished.

A further learning that endures is the capacity to see group behavior from a new perspective. An important sensitization to the whole nonverbal communication field seems to be enhanced in many family members, and this kind of awareness often carries over into other social groupings. The development of this kind of understanding of human behavior permits many people for the first time to realize their own behavior is not solely derived from within themselves, but rather is intimately related to the contexts in which they find themselves, and to the signals which are constantly being exchanged among any group. On the other hand, this very awareness combined with a knowledge of their own personal feeling reactions, which in the past have frequently been denied, opens for them the possibility of new autonomous, self-assertive behavior as individuals.

Special Effects

Earlier I noted that with additional equipment including several cameras, and a special effects generator, effects could be obtained which have additional therapeutic usefulness. Some of these can be obtained simply, and they will be included in this brief section.

The most simple, and yet one that is extremely effective, can be obtained by shutting off the sound and viewing only the action. In this manner, distracting words are eliminated and suddenly vivid, nonverbal messages may emerge from the gestures and movements in the family group. For example, during an argument, the actions of one member minus the words may seem to be utterly incongruous, with all the gestures and facial expressions indicating an obsequious submissiveness, while in the sound version the words bellow forth a seemingly frightening challenge.

Serial recordings are also extremely useful. These are obtained merely by saving short significant segments from ongoing sessions, and periodically showing the entire sequence. The changes in behavior over the time span often are startling, and can give added incentive to people to continue the process of change. The replay of such a sequence is especially valuable when some member feels discouraged and has the subjective feeling that nothing has been accomplished.

The videotape technique can be combined with other special methods, and can add to their effectiveness. For example, when gestalt techniques are used and taped, replay often provides additional impact and insight. Videotaping role-playing is another instance where the playback adds enormously to the effectiveness of the experience.[7]

The impact of seeing one's own image can be made an even more profound experience by using certain self-confrontation adaptations. The original one was described by Tausig and Schaeffer.[10] In this method, an individual is seated directly in front of a TV monitor, and a full-face image from a camera directly behind the monitor is shown on the screen. The individual is asked to imagine that the image on the screen is another person, and he is requested to hold a dialogue with that person. The image is then addressed by the therapist and told to reply to the actual subject. In this way a dialogue is established, and frequently very personal feelings of self are revealed as they are projected back and forth. Further elaborations of this method, including the projection on a split-screen of both profiles of a person's face, have been described more fully in another of the present author's papers.[2]

Still other useful effects can be obtained with video recorders that allow for slow motion, still-framing, and fast motion. The slow motion can catch the initiation of behavioral sequences, and also can capture the shifting flow of a series of facial expressions, e.g., the shift from interest, to doubt, to condescension. The still-frame allows a person to associate to one expression that may have lasted for only a fraction of a second, yet which may contain the most revealing nuance in explaining a complicated behavioral sequence. Fast motion, on the other hand, may be extremely useful in condensing time so that behavior not ordinarily recognized at the regular rate of speed becomes meaningful when seen in this altered mode. A couple who appear unremarkable in conversation together take on new meaning when in fast replay it is seen that the husband moves so little that even in this rapid mode he still appears motionless; the wife on the other hand in the fast mode now seems to be frantically moving her hands and twisting her body. In such an actual case, the wife for the first time became aware of her frustration and her desperate feeling of futility as she sought in vain to evoke some response from her extremely passive husband.

Finally, special effects can be used to show large pictures of two members on a split-screen, side-by-side, even though in the actual room setting they may be across from one another. In this way, sensitive mirroring behavior indicating the synchrony and closeness of alliance between the two can be startlingly demonstrated. By similar technical means, the entire family can be shown with a superimposition of the face of one member on the screen. This has been used with profound effect in a family where one member holds the power to control the mood of the entire group. In the picture, this member is seen encompassing everyone, and since facial expression is frequently used to convey mood, the depressed features of the controlling member overshadowing everyone is evocative of an intense awareness in everyone of just who dominates the family scene.

COMMENT

The qualities of videotape have been highlighted to emphasize the unique value of immediate playback in family therapy. For the first time therapists now have a way to feed back pertinent objective data from a therapy situation so that the effect can be immediately reflected in the ongoing process. In addition, because the data provided are equally available to family members and therapist alike, a situation that encourages a more equal and democratic relationship among therapist and patients is encouraged.

Finally, because the new cassette video-recorders are both economical and reliable, and because their portability and ease of operation make them mechanically feasible for even the most technically doubtful therapist, it is anticipated that the use of video recordings as an adjunct in family therapy will become increasingly popular, and the value of such methods more widely appreciated.

REFERENCES

1. Alger I: Therapeutic use of videotape playback. J Nerv Ment Dis 148:430–436, 1969

2. Alger I: Television image confrontation in group therapy, in Sager CJ, Kaplan H (eds): Progress in Group and Family Therapy. New York, Brunner/Mazel, 1972

3. Bateson G, Jackson DD, Haley J, et al: A note on the double-bind. Fam Process 2:154–162, 1963

4. Berger M (ed): Videotape Techniques in Psychiatric Training and Treatment. New York, Brunner/Mazel, 1970

5. Bodin A: The use of video-tapes, in Ferber A, Mendelsohn M, Napier A, (eds): The

Book of Family Therapy. New York, Science House, 1972

6. Cornelison FS Jr, Arsenian J; A study of the response of psychotic patients to photographic self-image experience. Psychiatr Q 34: 1–8, 1960

7. Goldfield M, Levy R: The use of television videotape to enhance the therapeutic value of psychodrama. Am J Psychiatry 125: 690–692, 1968

8. Paul N: Self and cross-confrontation techniques via audio and visual tape recordings in conjoint family and marital therapy. Presented at 45th Annual Meeting, American Orthopsychiatric Association, Chicago, Ill, March 1968

9. Stoller FH: Use of videotape (focused feedback) in group counseling and group therapy. J Res Develop Educ 1 (2):30–44, 1968

10. Tausig TN, Schaeffer S: Self-image experience by immediate television feedback: A preliminary report. Unpublished

Multiple Family Therapy: Questions and Answers

H. Peter Laqueur, M.D.

MULTIPLE FAMILY THERAPY is an adaptation of group techniques to the treatment of families. As such, it has considerable potential as a clinical and public health procedure. Establishing such groups is comparatively safe and easy; yet, they seem bewildering to the beginner. This article, using a question and answer format, will present the history and rationale of MFT as well as the steps by which such groups can be established.

What is Multiple Family Therapy?

Five or six families are brought together in a room with the declared intent to have repeated such sessions lasting from 60–75 min, in which the families will share problems with each other as well as models and suggestions for problem solving. The therapist acts as the "conductor" of this small orchestra of 20–25 people, and may be assisted in this work by a cotherapist, often several observers (therapy trainees), video camera men, and one or more supervisors who co-experientially share the room where the sessions take place.

What are the origins of MFT as a specific technique?

The term "multiple family therapy" was created by Carl Wells in 1963, when we published our first paper. During the 10 yr previous to that, we had brought families together, teaching them to help each other. This actually began in 1951 with a unit of 17 patients, who were receiving insulin therapy. Families became angry with the doctor when he talked only with the patients separating them from their family's understanding; patients became angry when he only talked with the families who then seemed to be in collusion with the established authority. We concluded it would be best to bring them all together to explain what the treatment process was. This was the beginning of MFT, although we had not named it as such yet.

The first meeting planned for about 15 min at the end of visiting hours on a Sunday afternoon took 45 min because of the many questions that were being asked. It continued with the families standing out on the grass outside of the hospital talking to each other for another half hour. This never had happened before because usually the families visiting patients in a state hospital were ashamed to face each other.

What physical equipment is required?

Any large, acoustically acceptable and decently ventilated room in which thirty chairs can be placed in a circle (with some pillows in the middle if desired) is suitable to accommodate five to six families and a therapy team for 75 min. Special props are not required; a blackboard may be useful if someone wants to explain an interrelation problem, but a sketch block and a black marker can fulfill the same purpose.

Reprint requests should be addressed to H. Peter Laqueur, M.D., 43 Randall Street, Waterbury, Vt. 05676.

Video is highly desirable but can occasionally be dispensed with if therapists can teach observers and "advanced families" to describe to the group
the nonverbal exchanges they perceive. For training and for research, video
appears to be as necessary as a microscope is for the study of histopathology
and microbiology.

In our Vermont State Hospital studio, we have an adjacent video control
room with large windows looking into the treatment rooms. Families with
anywhere from three to eight family members (parents, one or two grandparents, several children) seat themselves in a large ellipse with therapist,
co-therapist, and two or more observer-trainees. Thus, up to 30 people may
be observed working together. Good lighting is provided to enable two camera
operators, connected with headphones and throat microphones with the clinically sophisticated video director's desk in the control room, to scan and
record whatever movements the participants make and to "zoom-in" on special
situations.

Less elaborate arrangements work perfectly well. It is not necessary for
example, to have such a complicated video facility unless the production of
training and research tapes is contemplated. The inclusion of a simple video
set-up (see Alger) is highly recommended however and the general size of the
group described seems quite workable. MFT meetings may take place in a
hospital, a library, a TV studio or in a clinic, a- doctor's office, or even at
several different times in various family homes. It is important that one be
aware of the different effects of such different environments on the group as
a whole, on its members, and on the therapy and observation teams. Above
all, it is important to avoid excessive structure and to give the participants
a feeling of flexibility and adaptability. Accepting small disturbances, phone
calls, heat and light changes, and unusual noises can do this. Members
come late and are permitted to leave unexpectedly. An angry young child may
scream or fall to the floor leading other mothers to intervene and help.
While the sessions are task oriented, we aim for a feeling of freedom so that
members can express themselves rather than hold back under rigid authoritarian rules.

It should be remembered that many MFT groups are made up of severely
disorganized, socially and psychologically disadvantaged families, who are
quite unaccustomed to self-examination or self-expression, especially in the
setting of such institutions as large hospitals and clinics.

How are groups selected and organized?

Families referred to our unit are randomly distributed according to available openings in several co-existing therapy groups. They are briefly told
that we do not believe in "primary patient" versus "healthy" family members
but that we like to deal with disturbed interaction patterns in the entire
family in order to help them all. They are invited to sit in with an existing group,
are introduced, and, in most instances, they begin to participate immediately.
We try to make MFT groups as random as possible in their socioeconomic
as well as their ethnic, religious, political and age characteristics. The more
one selects families for any specific factor, e.g., psychiatric diagnosis, intelligence, economic status, and special interests, the higher the probability

of pseudo-intellectuality and of superficial discussions around so-called "common interests."

Groups meet at least once a week for 75 min, usually in the evening hours on the same weekday. A beginning group may meet three to five times within a 2-wk period then taper off to one meeting per week. We see no advantage in meeting fewer than three to four times per month, although some groups in New York have made slow but significant progress with two monthly meetings only, over a 3–4 yr period.

Some families attend all meetings with rare absences of one of the members. Many families attend all meetings but with varying absenteeism of one or more members; a few families attend irregularly and may drop out only to return later when they see that they can use this form of therapy.

Families from differing cultures and from different social strata in the same culture are brought together in these groups. Is this workable and by what reasoning is this so?

Each culture and time period has its own, more or less bell-shaped, curve of families, which it defines as ranging from "very sick" to "very healthy." If we could average all American or Western European families, we could in a more general sense define that noncommunication or double-binding, for example, are pathologic. The specific sexual, religious, and political metaphors associated with isolation and withdrawal might be very different in different cultures. One may feel free to discuss a specific subject with one family, while another family might recoil from mention of a remotely related issue.

Our *basic assumption* is this: No matter what culture, social setting, or time period a family finds itself in, there are basic human behavior patterns that can help people to grow and live creatively, while there are others that lead to stunted growth, mutual fear, evasive and noncommunicative actions, and eventual breakdown and sickness in one or several family members.

We do not attempt to treat the sick individual, but we wish to detect sickness-provoking mutual behavior in families. We aim to let the families themselves discover such patterns with us, so that families may act as co-therapists and teach each other possibilities for change, for coping with problems in a new way.

It is evident that the great variety of value systems in five to six different families would lead to fruitless debates if specific behavioral issues were taken up as topics. Some families would feel "right" about their solution, while others might think of them as being "dead wrong." Acerbities, mutual recrimination, calumniating allegations, and name calling would be the order of the day, and no new insights or changed behavior could develop.

It is the therapist's task to prevent such fruitless discussions. He must provide the MFT group with necessary information for their work on a deeper level. Thus, he provides descriptive information relating to such things as hurt expressions, signs of rejection or rebellion, and of intolerance; he attempts to elicit feelings and make those that are covert manifest. Finally, he aims to locate and display for the group the dyadic and triadic alliances and counter-alliances that are continually forming and reforming. The final goal of this is that group members become aware of these issues so that they are able to

understand each other on the deeper human levels that bridge cultural differences.

An important feature of the value and cultural issue concerns the degree to
which sub-groups within the culture, e.g., fathers, mothers, adolescent boys,
adolescent girls, and so on, have special interests and ways of experiencing
life that cannot simply be understood by individuals not belonging to that sub-
group. The MFT group allows first for formulation of the experience of
frustration and deprivation within any of these groups and subsequently leads
to better understanding and solving of the issues of such differences. An
example would be the identification constellation between mothers whose
daughters have accused them of being inadequate or insensitive or imper-
ceptive. This frequently can be used therapeutically by relating it to the generational experience of the mothers when they were daughters themselves.

How does the session proceed?

Most people in the room know each other already from previous sessions,
with the exception perhaps of one *new* family. New families are admitted to
replace those that have ceased to participate either because they recovered
or—in about 10% of the cases—because they dropped out and could not be
retrieved. There may also be a trainee or observer, who is being introduced
to the older members of the MFT group.

The therapist usually starts off by asking whether the group wishes to pur-
sue a previous topic or whether anyone feels the need to start on something
new. After this has led to a decision on the topic, by the suggestion of one
or more members, the group talks in spurts for a little while until the therapist or co-therapist describes the first *common denominator* that the beginning
discussion seems to contain, e.g., the complaint of a mother about the irre-
sponsibility of her daughter (coming home late, etc.). The therapist may point
out that "there are several mothers in this room, who have felt unhappy about
their daughters' behavior—so perhaps it might be useful to talk about the attitudes of mothers and daughters toward each other. Some do not seem to live
peacefully and happily with each other—what might be causing this? What
could be done about it?"

This takes the group further away from specific value systems and moral or
social issues into the deeper field of mother–daughter and parent–child emotional relations, providing an opportunity for the whole group to become involved in terms of their own emotional anxieties and frustrations.

After 15–20 min of such group activity, the therapist may cause a break in
the discussion by asking, "Shall we review what we have done so far?"—
or by suggesting that the group view together the video tape that has been made
in order to give people a chance to see and comment on their behaviors in
interaction. The instant replay capability of television is obviously an advantage here. After such a verbal review, or video review, the group is usually
ready for a more active intimate description and examination of feelings and
attitudes. Throughout this part of the session, group members may sometimes
change positions; instead of sitting together clustered as individual families, a
mother may take a seat next to another mother, a father may move close to
another father, youngsters may have found each other sitting on pillows in the

middle of the room or in a special far corner of the ellipse. There is a lively give and take going on between some members, while others may look silent, even glum and morose or angry, but hardly ever bored.

After 20–30 min, the therapist may request the co-therapist to sum up "what has happened today." The co-therapist may do this, or perhaps point out that some group members had been left out and should be given a chance to speak. After an additional 10 min or so of this the group breaks up slowly after agreeing with the therapist on the place and time for the next meeting.

Three phases of MFT are being described. What are they?

In *Phase I,* individuals are only vaguely aware of the fact that their own behavior may have invited response patterns that caused them to become fearful, disgusted, rejected, and emotionally abandoned. In the group, members come to see each other as suffering or joyful human beings, rather than as walking, rather cruel, information centers. This produces an initial sense of relief in group members who have suffered rejection and misunderstanding in their families and now see that something is about to be done about it. They may also develop an initial sense of some personal capability for improving their lives. To some degree there is a kind of magical relief due to unreal expectations. But there is also a chance to observe other suffering (and improving) families at first hand, and to have a spark of hope kindled.

Phase II (resistance to treatment) occurs when a creeping understanding appears on the horizon, that a change of attitude and behavior is required not only in those who misunderstand and reject, but also in the individual himself who (for 1001 good reasons) behaves in such a way that misunderstanding and rejection come about.

Depending on the severity of interactional disturbance patterns, and the length of time in the patient's previous life over which they developed, the second or resistance phase may take anywhere from 2–24 mo (with an average required period from 12–14 mo) before change in the emotional response patterns based on something more than willingness to give lip service to therapeutic suggestions can be obtained. All individuals concerned must first gain confidence that risk-taking, reaching out to the other person, or expressing anger rather than repressing such feeling can be safe, and that the other person may respond positively rather than with withdrawal, irrelevancy, or rejection. When all concerned with previous negative behavior have thus gained more courage (and have become willing to be less "innocent," "good," while making the other person look like a "villain"), then Phase II can slide slowly into Phase III, where people begin to teach others by model and analogy. The need for constant defense and the need to sabotage the therapeutic process subsides. Thus, in Phase III, learning by analogy, by modeling and indirect interpretation occurs.

Can specific behavioral changes be associated with these phases?

Yes. *Phase I* behavior constitutes displays of *"emotional relief."* Treatment has begun and "something is being done about a painful situation."

Phase II behavior is characterized by hesitation, and reluctant cooperation with the treatment process. Families in this phase are often argumentative, doubt that "anyone ever changes," fear "to lose inner security and whatever little good relation they have" if they open up and confront the "sleeping dogs" in their lives.

Phase III shows true openness, increased self confidence, acceptance of some faults ("you can't win them all!") and helpfulness to other families in distress.

What is meant by learning by analogy?

A father can learn about paternal behavior by observing other fathers in action (and either approve or disapprove of the noticed results), as can a mother from other mothers, and a youngster from youngsters in other families. *Within the same family there are no useful analogies.* Jimmy, a youngster can point out to Tommy, another youngster, how Tommy's parents affect him, and from the discussion Jimmy's own parents can learn quietly without directly being confronted in open attacks.

How can one sick family serve as a healing model for another family?

If an MFT group discusses the processes that have led to sickness in Johnny's family, Tommy's family may learn to avoid some of the patterns that have led to trouble for Johnny and his parents. Naturally, two families are never exactly comparable, nor are two processes ever fully alike. Nevertheless, they may contain elements, which, when changed or avoided, can lead to improvement and better understanding. "Yesterday's pain may lead to today's understanding and thus to hope for tomorrow." (Poster in *Psychology Today,* November 1972.)

What is learning by indirect interpretation?

An example of *direct* interpretation would be the therapist saying to a patient, "You behave this way because you hate your father." The patient would nod his head, be very proud of his sophisticated insight, and then build inner defenses against this unacceptable idea that might require many months of therapy to overcome.

If the therapist had described to the group, in much more general indirect terminology, that "there seems to be people around whose inner growth can be hampered by their hidden hate for a parent," our patient, and others, might have been able to learn by self-examination without the need of defense against open confrontation.

What are some typical problems in the conduct of a group?

Over-identification: If several persons take on an emotional problem simultaneously and intensely, it may be hard for others to express their feelings.

Me-too-ism is the confession of small sins, such as minor stealing, in order to avoid discussion of worries over the patient's own sexual performance.

Dumping is the process whereby people gang up on a victim in the group and add to other people's criticisms and accusations of him in an effort to avoid their own painful material. It is important to recognize that "dumping" is a collaborative and collusive process, which the victim frequently invites in order to help deal with guilt in himself.

Scapegoating: This process, so common in all natural systems, can go on in multiple family therapy groups as well. Essentially, what happens here is that a *systems* issue is dealt with by blaming a *single* individual and assigning to him responsibility for distress or malfunction in the entire system.

Escape into irrelevant discussions: The principal maneuver here is to avoid the target issue, whatever it may be. The other subject may have the appearance of being significant and important, but in fact it is brought up as a diversionary issue. Usually one discovers this by monitoring the flow of process in the group and by becoming aware of the switch from the central topic to some attractive but irrelevant issue. Usually hot issues, such as politics or religion, serve best as red herrings.

Playing down the importance of emotional events is effected to avoid a real change in attitude. For example, "I used to be afraid of mother's scorn—now I have learned to avoid such scenes." As can be seen, the issue has not really been dealt with, except by avoidance.

Token emotional reaching out with subsequent long withdrawal occurs when the risk of being rejected turns out to be too high. Frequently, as the move toward the other person is being made, the withdrawal route is already being prepared. Thus, the move becomes a token rather than a committed effort towards involvement.

Using secret codes, verbal or nonverbal known only to family members, which convey information to someone in the family, is designed to close off discussion of a dangerous area. Families have had a lifetime of opportunity to learn each others' signals, and these are not readily understood by a therapist. Often other families are more effective at breaking these codes and are able to help because of their own experience. At such moments, the therapist may feel confused, bewildered, and unable to understand the direction things are taking, because he is unaware of the secret meaning of these messages. In such circumstances the therapist can assist in circumventing this defensive process, by insisting on discovering the real meaning of the transactions taking place, often with the aid of explanations by other families.

How can individual crises in the group be handled?

(1) By direct support from therapist or co-therapist, e.g., encouragement with a show of warmth, interest, and understanding. In more serious instances, it may be useful occasionally for one of the therapy team to take a person aside individually and speak with him or her alone in another part of the room for a few moments. This would be out of the range of the cameras and out of range of hearing, but would at the same time be visible to the entire group.

(2) By encouraging group members to give support, again by expression of reassurance and understanding.

(3) The flight of a group member from the room poses a problem for the therapist. If anger and withdrawal are being used in an exploitive or manipulative way, often the most useful way of dealing with them is to allow the person to leave, in effect, to call his bluff. On the other hand, people leaving in a sense of overwhelming and genuine distress and pain or despair need the support that comes with staying with them. Here, the most desirable way of dealing with the situation involves having one of the therapy team, or one of

the group members, accompany the person out of the room, stay with him, and often return to the group with him. At times, it is useful to interfere firmly with the move to leave. This alone is often reassuring enough to redirect the work in a therapeutic direction.

(4) By ignoring the crisis for the moment (letting matters rest and cool off) and then giving support and descriptive analysis later.

(5) By encouraging the group to reflect and report the emotions aroused and make suggestions as to what should be done.

What if the family refuses to come?

We can call on them, telephone, send a teamworker, or a friend from the family group to find out what happened. If the reason for staying away is due to some clinical error, such as inattention to the family, or provocative behavior by the group or therapy team, the family may be invited "with apologies" to return and openly discuss their anger or disappointment.

Therapists must model their willingness to admit to mistakes and make amends, without becoming excessively self-accusatory and masochistically submissive.

What if the family monopolizes the stage?

Here, video playback, or interruption by the therapist to ask the group to describe "what is going on," is most helpful. Very often, one or the other of these simple devices helps to restore the balance, or to mobilize other families to interfere actively with the monopolization.

Suppose material from one family is too threatening for the group because it is too primitive, or too violent and sexual in nature?

We have always been amazed how much the families can take, once a group member has brought up highly emotional-charged material. There may be some initial warding off, escape talk, giggling, or intellectualization. The next meeting after a "hot and heavy" or "fearful and belligerent" session may sound very conventional and dull, as if there were a reluctance to continue dealing with the charged material. However, invariably in such a dull session, someone expresses regret and the wish to return to the emotional field where real progress can be made. That does happen one or two sessions later, and then "work through" processes have clearly begun.

How is home visiting and individual psychotherapy used in conjunction with MFT?

These methods are complementary; if a person is too shy or reticent in the group, a few individual encouraging sessions may be most helpful. If someone has a secret that he dare not reveal, the significance of such a problem may have to be explored in individual approaches. The ultimate goal remains: To better honest relationships between family members as self-confidence increases.

The home visit (see Bloch) is a most useful data-gathering tool that we are using to an increasing degree. We think that in the past we worked too often in the blind and could have done much better if we could have been more aware of the circumstances of the families' lives.

How do the effects of MFT differ from those of other group procedures, such as peer group therapy, conjoint family therapy, and network therapy?

Peer group therapy.   In peer groups, the family of each patient is present in fantasy only. The rejections, fears, and doubts that patients report and compare with each other are often distorted through unconscious irrational forces. MFT allows patients to compare their fellow patients' statements with observable realities and can thus lead to increase in reality assessments and testing.

Conjoint family therapy.   Conjoint therapy with the single family compares to MFT as individual therapy compares to peer group therapy. It is helpful but requires that the patient must later learn from others how external settings affect other families differently than his own family. Most often, families with a hospitalized member are severely isolated and do not have much opportunity to learn from social contact about other adaptive and interactional modes. MFT provides a safe place for this to happen.

Network therapy.   As practiced by Speck and Attneave,[7] this involves bringing together fifty or more people in social and kin networks.

Network therapy has many advantages, although the absence of analogous family situations here (with other parents, grandparents, siblings), leaves some reality aspects in doubt. Furthermore, as a practical basis, large networks are hard to bring together and it is difficult in our culture (in contrast, for example, to the American Indians) to solve the logistic and economic problems of bringing together such large groups. Multiple family therapy groups are easy to arrange.

What contraindications are there to the use of MFT?

Very few. Occasionally one must wait and do some individual and conjoint single family therapy to prepare peoples' willingness to engage in gradual open discussion of "skeletons in the closet" with others who have had similar hesitations. If another person besides the primary patient is very unstable and likely to become sick dramatically before the family has fitted itself in the MFT process, some precautionary help for that person may also be required.

What general theory does MFT operate under?

Each open (living) system, whether it be an individual, a small group, a family, an MFT group, an agency or institution, a community, a nation, or all of humanity depends for its survival on orderly processing of input data, on efficient selection of relevant information and on decision making and an effective output of actions, the results of which must be fed back for assessment, correction, and adaptive future action. Any friction or malfunction between component parts, including decrease in the discriminatory power of internal and external sensors leads to decreased efficiency and survival capability.

A *family* in order to survive must be able to perceive and head off external dangers (physical and biologic, political, economic), as well as internal frictions (paralyzing quarrels, mutual put-downs and discouragement) in order to maintain its stability. If we detect processes that interfere with survival abilities, we can alter them by describing them in general terms to the family, and assist them in correcting the malfunction before it becomes fatal. A delay at the feedback loop, for instance can cause people to overlook warning signals and go through danger signals unheeded, while a faster perception of such dangers could help to avoid collisions with threatening factors in the external milieu.

General systems theory has directed our attention to phenomena within the family and the therapy group that would have otherwise escaped our attention, e.g., the handling of overloads through bypass techniques, and the impairment and restoration of external and internal signal sensitivities. We now understand the possibility of producing a focus of excitation and interest that can spread through the whole system thus generating insights in many individuals who otherwise might have been left behind or on the sidelines. With application of the principle of reverberating (circular) interaction between therapist and group members, a pace of therapeutic progression becomes possible that linear, "cause-effect," techniques could never have produced.

How are people trained to do MFT?

People who are to learn to do MFT should be familiar with the rich literature and techniques in the areas of conjoint family therapy, network therapy, individual therapy, and peer group therapy. We train future multiple family therapists (1) to detect and recognize features of the affective rather than the cognitive exchanges across interfaces and boundaries; (2) to identify with hostility and rage, seductiveness, anxiety and fear, hopelessness, frustration, perplexity, and abandonment; and (3) to point this out to individuals and to identification constellations among group members, so that what the 20–25 individuals have in common in the way of feelings and attitudes becomes more important to them than what they "know" or "do not know."

As noted earlier, most sessions include observers and trainees, usually seated in an outer ring around the central working group. Trainees sit in and listen for a number of sessions and write observations of sessions, which are openly read and discussed in training sessions with the other trainees. They observe each other and are observed by supervisors who sit in with them while they do co-therapy. Many sessions are video-taped with discussions of the playback and emphasis on different levels of observation and participation and on awareness of the difference between the two. Trainees spend considerable time observing each other.

Of critical importance are descriptions of their own family development, and sessions during which trainees discuss and sculpt (see Duhl) their own families.

Can the general practitioner and psychiatric generalist safely establish multiple family therapy groups?

The general practitioner should understand from this that he is dealing with a format and a technique that fall within the sphere of his own competence. If he and his office nurse or social worker establish a multiple family therapy group and observe some simple rules, they can safely begin an exploration of their own capabilities in this area and begin to help patients by this mode. The first rule would be not to take sides, to recognize that all interactions are essentially symmetrical and fair, and represent the best efforts of all of the participants. For example, as we have noted earlier, the scapegoat is an active participant in his own scapegoating and invites this for reasons of his own.

In addition he must try as best he can to be sensitive and perceptive to the needs of *all* of the members of the group, not only those of the index patient.

Finally, he should recognize and admit his own limitations and, thus, look for help from more experienced and presumably more competent professionals when things get out of hand. This implies a continuous process of testing his own skills and his own capacity to grow. It should be noted that the multiple family therapy group format has many built-in safety features, that the dangers are minimal, and that the opportunities for improving performance are very substantial.

The motto of the entire transaction is to teach families to help each other.

REFERENCES

1. Laqueur HP: General systems theory and multiple family therapy, in Masserman JH (ed): Current Psychiatric Therapies, vol 8, New York, Grune & Stratton, 1968

2. Laqueur HP: Mechanisms of change in multiple family therapy, in Sager CJ, Kaplan HS (eds.): Progress in Group and Family Therapy, New York, Brunner/Mazel, 1972, p. 400

3. Laqueur HP: Multiple family therapy and general systems theory. Int Psychiatry Clin 7:4, 99, 1970

4. Laqueur HP: Systems therapy, in Masserman, JH (ed): Current Psychiatric Therapies, vol II. New York, Grune & Stratton, 1971

5. Laqueur HP, LaBurt HA, Morong E: Multiple family therapy: Further developments. Int J Soc Psychiatry Congress issue, special edition, No. 2, Section K, 1964, pp 69 80

6. Laqueur HP, Wells CF, Agresti M: Multiple family therapy in a state hospital. Hosp Community Psychiatry 20:13–20, 1969

7. Laqueur, HP: Systems therapy, in Masserman JH (ed): Current Psychiatric Therapies, vol 11. New York, Grune & Stratton, 1971, pp 52–55

Marriage Therapy in a Couples Group

James L. Framo, Ph.D.

THERE IS LITTLE QUESTION that marriage as a social institution is in a severe crisis at this time. It has been estimated that, when the statistics are examined carefully, about half of all current marriages are ending in divorce; in some parts of the country the divorce rate exceeds the marriage rate. Taking into account the number of married people who stay together unhappily, we can understand that some people question the viability and workability of the marriage state and experiment with "living together" and forming group and multi-person marriages.

A more balanced view of marriage is not as pessimistic as the foregoing suggests. There are many positive sides to a marriage relationship that are not observable to outsiders, even to marriage therapists. One certainly cannot tell how a marriage is doing by how the husband and wife behave with each other in social situations; unless one knows otherwise, people assume that other people's marriages are working. It is true, in a sense, that the public reports given out about one's marriage are like the communiques issued by heads of state after an international meeting: Neither one tells you very much about what is really going on.

A realistic view of marriage, based on intimate knowledge of a couple, has to recognize not only the cliché that "all marriages have problems," but that in the course of a marriage over time *every* marriage has *serious* problems to the point where divorce or separation is at least considered.

In examining some of the dynamics involved in mate selection and the relationship between marriage partners, we note that people are usually unaware of their own secret agendas when they marry, partially because these unconscious designs are clouded by their conscious goals: romantic love and sexual attraction (which, by the way, have an essential validity in their own right and should not be discounted).[7] Because of conflicts hanging over from the family of origin, people often marry those with whom they can prove or correct something, or those who will fill gaps in their own personality; they marry those who will punish them or whom they can punish, or those who will enable them to continue or master old conflictual relationships. There is some evidence, too, that people marry those who will help them to replicate or improve on their family of origin.[9] Many people believe that marriage should provide a solution to their personal problems, or at least provide an escape from an intolerable situation in their family of origin. The discrepancy between the conscious and unconscious demands placed on marriage, then, helps to explain why untroubled marital integration is the exception rather than the rule.

After the initial euphoria of togetherness in the early months of the new marriage, some disappointment is inevitable. Each partner unconsciously at-

Reprint requests should be addressed to James L. Framo, Ph.D., Jefferson Medical College, 1234 Locust Street, Philadelphia, Pa. 19107.

tempts to maneuver the other into some earlier relationship pattern in the family of origin; each has the disquieting feeling that some old, tormenting ghost has risen to haunt him. The marriage, seriously entered into with such dreams, hopes, and expectations for happiness, often begins to sound like a broken record from the past, even to the point where some of the same lines from the script will be repeated. A wife, for example, may hear herself repeating the same words she heard her mother use with her father during an argument, or the husband may use his father's coping methods of bitter silence or leaving the house to get drunk.

Many people are unable to make a genuine emotional commitment to the mate, other than to have fantasies of romantic fusion. The married person's primary loyalties and commitments may be to the family of origin rather than the mate. Sometimes the overriding loyalty to the original family is direct and obvious, as seen in complaints that in any showdown the spouse always sides with his own parents, brothers, or sisters. Sometimes the criticism is that the mate must see or talk to a parent or sibling every day on the telephone, or must live with or near a parent, or must give time, work, or money to his family of origin. Primacy of devotion to the family of origin over the current family or marriage can be present even when the person has little or no contact with his parents and considers himself liberated from them. Those adults who have cut themselves off from their family of origin are *even more likely* to act out with their mate and children the irrational hangovers from the past. In any event, out of the despair and outrage that the mate has not fulfilled a promise (to love, honor, obey, take care of, overlook, tolerate, care unconditionally, etc.) and out of the disappointment that the marriage did not make right what has always been wrong, spouses often turn to third parties to assuage their hurts. The third party, often triangulated to reduce tension in the marital twosome, can be a child, mistress or lover, liquor, hobbies, organizations, relatives, sports addictions, drugs, beauty parlors, or a psychotherapist.

RATIONALE FOR MARRIAGE THERAPY

Marital partners should be treated together, partly because, when a marriage is in serious trouble, the likelihood of divorce is greater if the partners go to two therapists separately, or if only one goes for treatment.[14] In treating a couple one must consider that there are three patients: the husband, the wife, and the relationship. Sometimes the relationship cannot be saved, in which event "divorce therapy" is done for partners who are truly allergic to each other (more about this later). Although marriage *counseling* has a long and respectable tradition, it should be distinguished from marriage *therapy,* a form of depth treatment, which not only deals with the intrapsychic dynamics of each spouse but also examines the interlocking nature of the marital bond. The motivational feedback system between husband and wife, moreover, occurs in the context of the whole family, including the children, as well as the extended family. It is not surprising, therefore, that many marriage therapists are basically family therapists who view human relationships in systems terms.

Experience with family therapy has indicated that the marriage relationship is the core of the family.[4] The greatest gift parents can give children is two adults with a secure sense of self who enjoy life and who have a viable relationship with each other characterized by love, sexual satisfaction, open communication, and mutual respect. Although most of the professional literature emphasizes the parent–child relationship in dealing with children's problems, family therapy experience has shown that the husband-wife axis is more critical to the welfare of the children. In many ways, it is much more difficult to be a mate than to be a parent. Whenever there is a disturbed child there is a disturbed marriage, although not all marriages in difficulty entangle or involve the children. Because of the interrelationship of parenting and marriage, most of the couples we have seen in marital therapy have come from family therapy that has progressed to the point where the originally symptomatic children no longer need treatment. Some couples, both with and without children, however, have started therapy explicitly because of marriage problems, in some instances because of open conflict, whereas other couples are estranged by silent warfare or by sexual dysfunctions. A few couples entered therapy to revitalize their "empty" relationships. Couples who have had successful marital therapy experiences often report that as their marriages improved, so did their children's problems, even in cases where the children were never seen in therapy.

A METHOD OF RUNNING A COUPLES GROUP

Married couples were originally put together into a treatment group for my own benefit—that is, in order to allow myself more therapeutic freedom to effect change. Although many couples utilized the conjoint marriage therapy setting most effectively and rehabilitated their relationship in a short period of time, other couples boxed me in by their triangulating efforts — e.g., insisting that I be judge or referee and decide who was right and who was wrong. Some couples moved for a while and bogged down; others developed such strong transference feelings that I was expected to be a super-parent and adopt them; and some couples were unable to stop fighting and listen to each other or the therapist. The idea of putting several of these difficult couples together in a group came from finding my own freedom of action blocked by my feelings of frustration, anger, and boredom. Although this step was originally taken for practical reasons of clinical expediency, it has had the serendipitous effect of demonstrating that couples group therapy is a powerful form of treatment in its own right. Based on experience with this method with over 200 couples, my belief is that couples group therapy is the treatment of choice for marital problems. (Incidentally, not all of the couples in treatment are married, but all have an ongoing relationship that the partners either want to make better, or feel they need help to terminate.)

Some of the reasons for the usefulness of couples group therapy are fairly obvious: Couples come to realize that their marital difficulties are not unique, and some marital relationships improve simply from recognizing how general marriage conflicts really are. (It is not uncommon for a couple leaving the first session to say, "My God, did you see *those* two! And I thought our marriage was bad.") In our culture, people do not get much opportunity to examine other people's marriages in depth. In the permissive, frank atmosphere of the group sessions, they can discover that every marriage has to work out accommodations in the universal areas of the handling of children, sex, money, and in-laws, and they learn that people are essentially more alike than different. They learn to use other marriage struggles as models of what to avoid or how things can be worked out. In this setting, spouses have a forum where the unrealistic expectations of marriage and of their mates can be exposed to the reality testing of the group. In a group context transference and counter-transference feelings are diluted, the therapist is less viewed as the rescuer, judge, persecutor, or all-loving parent, and the group process can be used for therapeutic leverage. Spouses can be stimulated to reconsider their own behavior by being exposed to contrasting patterns in other couples.

Often the individuals listen more to others in the group than they would to the therapist; people in the group, who do not have to take a therapist's stance, can confront someone in street language in such a way that the words have greater impact than a clinical interpretation. (For example, one woman in the group did not modify her bitter, attacking behavior toward her husband until another man in the group told her, "You're really a ball-breaking bitch. I sure would hate to be married to you.") In many ways, the group serves the supportive and confronting function for marriages that used to be served by extended family.

Couples group therapy as conducted by the present method does not bear much relationship to conventional peer group therapy, even though there is a similarity in the sense that a group of people are being treated together. Group therapy is based on an assemblage of strangers who have no past history with each other or likelihood of a future together. In couples groups, the marital unit has had a past history and is likely to have a future long after the group is disbanded (although, of course, the couples are strangers to each other initially). Consequently, in order of priority, we consider the individuals' first obligation to be to themselves, then to their mates, and only peripherally to the group. In my particular method of conducting these groups, I deemphasize the group process as such, although I am continually aware of it and use it to help bring about change. What is meant by this is that *there is not much focus on the relationships and distortions between individuals across couples.* For instance, the transference of a husband to someone else's wife who reminds him of his sister would not be worked with, whereas the transference distortions that occur between marital partners would be of paramount importance. However, the group process is used in various ways—by drawing contrasts between couples, by managing the time allotted to each couple, by dealing with group feelings when a couple is especially hostile to each other, or regresses, or has made much progress and is ready to terminate.

Usually, there are three couples in a group and sessions last for about an hour and a half; the focus is on one couple at a time, while the other two couples are instructed to attend carefully. The target couple is engaged rather actively; at the end of approximately 25 min each other person in the room is asked to give his or her reactions to what was observed. Although each couple usually gets about a half hour of time, there are occasions, such as when a particular couple is in an acute crisis, that the allotted times are made more flexible. This particular procedure of running couples groups owes a theoretical

debt to the work of M. Bowen, which emphasizes differentiation from the marital symbiosis as a primary goal of therapy. Bowen also pays much attention to the use of the self of the therapist in helping to bring about the development of a sense of self in each person in the group.[1]

The only criterion used for selection of couples for a particular group is age and stage of the life cycle. Couples who have recently married or have young children seem to do better with couples near their own age, whereas older married couples with adolescents or grown children tend to relate better to couples who are roughly in the same phase of the family. Couples are *not* selected on the basis of individual or marital psychopathology, social class, intellectual level, or any of the other conventional criteria. When dealing with intimate relationships people are reduced to the same level, whether the husbands and wives are Ph.D.s or housewives and plumbers. Often the lesser educated members of the group can zero in on an emotional level in a way that cuts right through the intellectualization of the more sophisticated members. Although some individuals have had a history of "mental illness" or hospitalization, this factor has not been a determining one in the progress they will make in this form of psychotherapy.

Most couples, who had been initially seen in either family therapy or conjoint marital therapy, are reluctant to enter a couples group. Sometimes there are valid secrets or skeletons in the closet that the partners do not want to reveal to others. Other times an individual will say, "I can't talk in front of other people," or "I'm not interested in other people's problems." Sometimes couples have been placed in groups after extensive periods of prior work; in other instances they have started with the group after only one initial interview as a single couple. More recently, having been impressed with the fairly rapid progress made with explicit marital problems in couples group therapy, we have put spouses in groups after only several therapy sessions as a couple alone. Those partners who are reluctant to join a group are encouraged to attend several sessions on a trial basis, with the option of going back to single couple therapy if it is felt that the group method is not productive. It is extremely rare for a couple to drop out of the group once having tried the experience. One husband, who entered the group unwillingly, with the warning, "O K , doc, I'll come, but I won't say a word when I get there," became the one member of the group whom we could not get to stop talking.

When I start a new group of three couples who are all meeting each other for the first time, I structure the beginning of the session with a few simple ground rules: (1) that a premium is placed on openness and honesty and the members are free to reveal themselves, their thoughts and feelings, but no physical violence is permitted; (2) that spouses are free to discuss the sessions afterwards, but should refrain from talking about the other couples in social situations where there might be other people present who know one of the other couples; and (3) that the members should try to make all criticisms of others in the group in a constructive fashion. My aim is to develop a safe, trusting atmosphere in this small society that does not operate with the social facades, and according to the rules of ordinary social behavior.

Once a group is started, it becomes open-ended—i.e., as couples terminate, new couples are added to the group. When one person cannot come to a session the partner is encouraged to come alone, to work on self. If a husband or wife drops out of treatment altogether, the mate is allowed to continue with the group if he or she is so motivated; this happens rarely. This procedure emphasizes the focus on autonomy and differentiation of self within the context of a relationship. Occasionally, the couples are seen with their children in family sessions, outside the couples group situation. This is done not only to get a reading on how the children are doing but also to evaluate how the whole family system is operating and to gauge the children's reactions to changes in their parents.

Most people enter marital therapy in order to change their mate; they are convinced that they are in the right, as any reasonable outsider would plainly see when the full story about the spouse is told, documented with specific examples. They believe that while there may be some petty quirks in their own personality, they would have no real difficulty becoming a good marriage partner if their mate would undergo some fundamental changes. Each married person secretly believes that his or her mate is seriously disturbed and cannot love. Individuals, as members of a marital unit, then, enter therapy with different hidden agendas as well as varying levels of motivation to change self, the mate, or to preserve the marriage. The couples who have the best prognosis, and who will make it with each other, are the ones who state, in essence, "We basically love each other and want to stay married, but for some reason we can't get along. Will you help us make this relationship work?" Some couples are on the verge of divorce and come to treatment as a last resort before consulting lawyers. It is rare, however, for couples to present their problems in joint fashion in these two ways—*both* wanting to continue or terminate the marriage. What is more common is that one partner is more explicitly discontented with the relationship. At the initial evaluation session, I suggest a period of exploratory therapy, with major decisions about the fate of the marriage being postponed until the partners can make more realistic and honest choices, based on the new knowledge and freedom that therapy can bring. When the negative emotional intensity is very high, I may suggest that a couple live apart from each other for a specified period, but that they continue to attend therapy sessions. These planned trial separations, suggested at various stages of the treatment according to the circumstances and the amount of mutual destructiveness, often help partners grow through the separation process and eliminate "if it weren't for you" games.[12]

One of the saddest and most difficult of situations to deal with in marital therapy is when one partner wants out of the marriage and the other desperately tries to hold on to the mate and grasps at any straw of hope to maintain the marriage. This circumstance is not always obvious in the beginning. Some people come to therapy with their mates as a token gesture; they may have someone else they want to marry but feel guilty about abandoning the mate. They agree to come to therapy so that later they can say they tried everything to "save" the marriage, and, besides, it would ease the conscience if the mate were left in the hands of the therapist. As soon as I become aware of this ploy and of the lip service being given to commitment to treatment, I expose it and suggest that honesty would be kinder in the long run. More commonly one partner is disturbed about the marriage relationship and the other, usually the husband, who came reluctantly in the first instance, does not feel their problems are unusual in kind or degree. He cannot understand what the fuss is all about. Men of this sort are uncomfortable when questioned and are loath to reveal feelings or anything "personal." Often this kind of man is difficult to involve in treatment until the therapist or the group provokes or challenges him. Not uncommonly, the wife discloses that because of his emotional neglect or indifference she has had an affair, a disclosure often followed by his becoming seriously upset. The differences in levels of awareness of a need for change of self, or the mate, or the desire to continue the marriage, provide the kind of heterogeneity that is useful for couples group therapy.

One of the reasons couples group therapy works rests on the truism that people can be much more objective about other people's problems than they can be about their own. It is not unusual during a session to witness an individual be active, perceptive, and right on target in his observations about someone in the group; as soon as he starts talking about himself, or his partner, there is a dramatic shift in tone of voice, his manner becomes hesitant, he blocks, and seems to be reduced to the functioning level of a mental defective. It is a sign of real progress when an individual gets to the point where he can get outside his own emotional field and view himself with objectivity.

When people start with a group, they are usually so preoccupied with their own distress that it is very difficult for them to attend to the problems of other couples, and it is an indication of movement when they can begin to be concerned about others. Members of the couples group are not always objective about others, however. Occasionally someone makes a very distorted observation about someone else, and it becomes necessary to modify this comment, or to check it out with the other members of the group. The therapist must be aware of this phenomenon of one forceful person projecting his or her own problem onto others under the guise of helpfulness. More difficult to detect and handle is the phenomenon of group irrationality. It is possible that an entire group can share a myth. (For example, if all three husbands are passive men who have lived by the formula of "peace at any price," they may be unanimous in the view that it is not necessary for men to take stands on issues. It is generally wise to have at least one vigorous male in a group.)

The mutually reinforcing defense systems or "games" that go on between married partners (e.g., one attacks and one defends, one over-functions and one under-functions, one is jealous and the other provokes jealousy) are quickly exposed in these groups. Each couple has its own style of interactional behavior, which is picked up rapidly by the other couples; these game-like patterns are repeated again and again until therapeutic change takes place. In this connection, a recurring event that takes the inexperienced therapist by surprise occurs when the spouse begins to change in the direction originally demanded by the partner and the partner not only seems indifferent to the change but even uncomfortable with it. This paradoxical reaction can occur, for example, when a formerly sexually unresponsive wife becomes more sexual, or when a silent husband begins to state his thoughts and feelings. Interestingly, partners often switch in their behavior, exchange symptoms, or shift positions on issues; a couple may start therapy with the husband wanting to rehabilitate the marriage and the wife wanting out, and the group is astonished when they reverse positions about the continuance of the marriage.

In general, most couples go through a predictable sequence as their repetitive interchanges undergo review by the reality testing of the group. Because of the premium placed on openness, early in the treatment the partners are apt to learn things about their mates that they never knew before; marital partners can be in the dark about what their mate really thinks even though they may have lived together for many years. Some of these disclosures can be shocking and painful, and one can sense the group discomfort when, for instance, a wife tells her spouse that she does not really love him or that he is not the real father of their daughter. Group anxiety can also rise when the hostility between partners becomes especially hurting and ugly. However, marital fighting can have a salutory effect on other couples, particularly those who had never had an open disagreement. "Pseudo-mutual" couples, that is, those who need to deny all differences, find it very difficult to maintain their illusion of compatibility when they are exposed to openly combative couples. One couple, who had never had an open argument with each other in 15 yr of marriage, had their first fight about another couple in the group while they were driving home from a couples group session. Interestingly, the 15-yr-old son of this couple, who had never had an open argument, had been arrested for fighting in school. This particular couple reported their joint fear that their first fight would lead to divorce. An important part of marital therapy consists of teaching couples who have never argued the value of learning how to confront and deal with issues between them. Bach's principles of "constructive fighting" are more useful for those fight-phobic partners than for the Virginia Woolf couples for whom insult-exchange is a ritualistic way of life.[9]

Most couples have an immediate and temporary positive response to the group and report after a few sessions that their marriage is much improved. However, another predictable stage of treatment, with some exceptions, is that, as they begin the work of therapy and as change threatens the system, there is usually some regression before they pull up again. One sign of improvement, even though it is accompanied by suffering and confusion, is when each partner becomes more individuated and there are more "I" position statements and fewer "*we* feel" or "*we* think" statements. The use of "we" is customary early in therapy because the expression conceals differences between the partners which might be frightening if revealed. A sense of personal identity, and respect for the partner's separate identity, is a critical ingredient in successful marital therapy; separateness of this order paradoxically brings about increased intimacy between the spouses.

Those couples who make considerable progress in the group often report that they feel really married for the first time; it is not unusual for older married couples to act like adolescents in love. Even though the other couples express their pleasure at seeing another couple "make it," and some are even spurred on to achieve the same state, there is also usually some envy and minor resentment as well as mourning when a couple leaves the group under these circumstances.

It should be mentioned that I do not discourage the couples in the group from having social contact outside the sessions. Indeed, some isolated couples made their first friends in the group. Often, the couples go to a restaurant together after meetings, rehash the sessions and gossip about the therapist and each other. Many couples have maintained friendships with each other long after the group has disbanded. However, in the many groups that I've seen there has never been an instance of extramarital sexual acting out between group members, although several couples in groups were involved in wife-swapping activities *outside* the group. (A few couples, on being invited to join the group, did have the fantasy that they were being invited into a sex, swinging group. One husband angrily said, "I want you to know that I don't go for that sort of thing.")

An atmosphere of discouragement can pervade sessions when one or more of the couples have a sense of hopelessness about their relationship; in this sense there can be group contagion. A shock wave of fear also runs through the group when a couple decide to divorce. When there has been intense emotional investment in each other, most partners cannot separate without bitterness, and a need for revenge. *Divorce therapy* is a relatively new therapeutic approach which is designed to help partners disengage from their relationship with a minimum of destructiveness to self, the mate, and the children, and with the freedom to form new relationships. The emotional turmoil surrounding such issues as child custody, visitation rights, and division of property are better handled in this therapeutic rather than legal atmosphere. The group can be of much help during this process of mutual recrimination and also in dealing with those situations where one partner is already out of the marriage and the other cannot let go until fault and blame has been dissipated as an issue. One couples group consisted of one couple in divorce therapy, one premarital couple trying to decide whether or not to marry, and one couple struggling to rehabilitate their marriage. In that particular group, the wife of the couple in divorce therapy dropped out of treatment, finished with the marriage, but her husband stayed on, and, with the help of the group, was finally able to achieve an "inner emotional balance," as he put it, before he was ready to give his wife an uncontested divorce.

Occasionally, "sibling rivalry" occurs between couples in the group. Until the group gets used to the format described in this paper, they are frustrated by the time limitations, and one person may state, "They got five minutes more than we did." It is true that if one couple is in an acute crisis they do get more time, but over a period of weeks the time allotted to each couple evens out. Besides, the couples soon learn that they can often get more out of observing the work being done with another couple than the time spent with them. The rivalry, furthermore, can be used to provide therapeutic leverage. For instance, if a couple is resistant and does not want to talk, I may say, "Well, I better move on to someone else. I can see you're not ready to deal with this." Couples handled in this manner are much more likely to be productive the next time their turn comes around.

At times, the therapist is accused of favoring or not liking men or women; as one may imagine, this creates lively discussions and smokes out hidden marital issues. Social movements such as women's rights or changes in sexual attitudes are interwoven with marital conflicts—a common example is the woman who wants to change her traditional housewife role and have an open marriage, or start a career. Because of these factors, as well as others, I have found that a heterosexual therapy team can run these couples groups more effectively than a solo therapist of either sex.

Since the relationship problems adults have with their mates and children are reconstructions and elaborations of earlier conflicts with the family of origin, I try to have at least one session with each adult and his family of origin, whether I am doing family, marital, or couples group therapy. Of all the treatment methods used, I find this the most powerful in terms of having an effect on the problems originally presented. The majority of adults are most reluctant to bring in their parents and siblings, often with the words, "Look, doc, you don't know how *impossible* my mother (or father) is." Some fear their parents will go crazy or die of a heart attack in the treatment session. Most of those who initially react negatively to the idea gradually come to see its value, especially when they see other individuals in the couples group do it and they hear about what was accomplished. These sessions with adults and their families of origin reveal important diagnostic information on how past family problems are being acted out in the present. More to the point, however, in these sessions opportunities are available for genuine corrective experiences and the clarification of old misunderstandings, providing a chance for adults and their parents to get to know each other as people. Many adults who have been cut off or alienated from their parents, sometimes for many years, find that when they have established more adult-to-adult relationships with their own parents and siblings they are able to relate to their spouses and children in a more adult manner.

Couples group therapy is not a new procedure, even though former publications on the topic have stressed quite different rationales and methods of running the groups.[3,5,6,8,10,11,13] This writer believes that there is great potential in this therapeutic method, and, as stated previously, that couples group therapy is probably the treatment of choice in dealing with marital problems. The consequences of marital stress, on children and society, are important enough to warrant further experimentation with this method and its techniques.

REFERENCES

1. Anonymous: Toward the differentiation of a self in one's own family, in Framo JL (ed): Family Interaction: A Dialogue Between Family Researchers and Family Therapists. New York, Springer, 1972

2. Bach GR, Wyden P: The Intimate Enemy: How to Fight Fair in Love and Marriage. New York, Morrow, 1969

3. Blinder MG, Kirschenbaum M: The technique of married couple group therapy. Arch Gen Psychiatry 17:44–52, 1967

4. Framo JL: Rationale and techniques of intensive family therapy, in Boszormenyi-Nagy I, Framo JL, (eds): Intensive Family Therapy. New York, Harper & Row, 1965

5. Gottlieb A, Pattison EM: Married couples group psychotherapy. Arch Gen Psychiatry 14:143–152, 1966

6. Hastings PR, Runkle RL: An experimental group of married couples with severe problems. Int J Group Psychother 13:85–92, 1963

7. Kubie LD: Psychoanalysis and marriage: practical and theoretical issues, in Eisenstein VW (ed): Neurotic Interaction in Marriage. New York, Basic Books, 1956

8. Leichter E: Group psychotherapy with married couples. Int J Group Psychother 12:154–163, 1962

9. Napier AY: The marriage of families: Cross-generational complementarity. Fam Process 10:373–395, 1971

10. Neubeck G: Factors affecting group therapy with married couples. Marriage and Family Living 16:216–220, 1954

11. Perelman JL: Problems encountered in psychotherapy of married couples. Int J Group Psychother 10:136–142, 1960

12. Toomin MK: Structured separation with counseling: A therapeutic approach for couples in conflict. Fam Process 11:299–310, 1972

13. Von Emde Boas C: Intensive group psychotherapy with married couples. Int J Group Psychother 12:142–153, 1962

14. Whitaker CA, Miller MH: A re-evaluation of "psychiatric help" when divorce impends. Am J Psychiatry 126:57–64, 1969

Managing Acute Psychiatric Emergencies: Defining the Family Crisis

Frank S. Pittman, III, M.D.

DESPITE WARNINGS against psychotherapists' communication with patients' relatives, it has been common practice, indeed a necessity, for psychiatric emergencies to be handled within the family context. Family therapy has certainly achieved its greatest acceptance in psychiatric emergency clinics and in the area of crisis intervention. It is not surprising that the most definitive documentation of the effectiveness of family therapy has been in the area of crisis and emergency treatment.

Langsley et al.,[7,8] in a controlled study of cases treated with family crisis therapy as an alternative to psychiatric hospitalization, showed that hospitalization was avoided in all but 19% of the experimental group during a 6-mo follow-up period. (*All* of the control group had been initially hospitalized for an average duration of 26 days, and during the 6-mo follow-up period 21% were readmitted.) On 18-mo and 3-yr follow-up, the experimental group was doing as well or better than the control group on various measures of functioning, symptoms, health, and family relationships. The mean days lost before returning to functioning, defined as resumption of usual role performance, was 72.5 days for the controls and only 25 days for the experimental group; cost of providing care for the control group was six and a half times as great for the control group as for the experimental, i.e., $1300 as against $200.

These procedures were described in a series of papers and books,[1-14] published from 1964–1971. Later, they were adopted for use in other settings: a busy general hospital emergency room, an affluent private practice, and a rural community mental health center. The specific techniques were modified in each setting, but the essential feature, the definition of the family crisis, remained central.

While the two tend to occur together, a distinction must be made between a crisis and an emergency. *Emergency is a subjective state*—a feeling that outside intervention is needed. Any outside intervention that comes immediately and removes responsibility from the overburdened person experiencing the emergency will be likely to reduce the runaway symptoms of emergency and thereby seems, however temporarily, to be therapeutic. Crisis is a more subtle concept —it may occur without all the turmoil of a subjective emergency state. It involves a process of systems change, is far more objective, and is not something to be relieved but something to be solved. The associated subjective emergency may be relieved by medicine, love, soothing words, or distracting activity, but the crisis is solved only by a process of definition and change. *Defining the family systems crisis* is the central process in managing acute breakdown,

Reprint requests should be addressed to Frank S. Pittman, III, M.D., 960 Johnson Ferry Road N.E., Suite 543, Atlanta, Ga. 30342.

whether accompanied by a sense of emergency or not. It may even be assumed, until otherwise demonstrated, that any request for intervention, however calm, may be an attempt at resolving a current crisis.

Crisis itself may be defined as the state of things in a system at a time when a change is impending. The family, as the basic social unit, continually monitors change over the lifetime of its members. The family must maintain its stability through life's changes, each of which may be a crisis. While it buffers its members against undesired or abrupt change, the family must prepare for and even force changes on its members, and on itself, as an integrated system. As the family is the social institution with the primary responsibility of both instituting and softening the change process, it both creates and resolves crisis, the state of impending change.

As outlined by Langsley, Kaplan, Pittman, Machotka, Flomenhoft, and DeYoung, family crisis therapy has seven phases, which overlap rather than succeed each other.

First is the therapist's *immediate availability*. He must give an emergency response, answering the call for immediate aid and acknowledging the intensity of the family's concern and current helplessness. This does not mean accepting the family's definition of the crisis or the emergency solutions they are proposing, but it does mean a willingness to listen and be involved.

Second is the therapist's insistence upon seeing the problem as *involving the family*. It is not always possible to treat the family, or even to meet with all the involved relatives, separately or together, but they are included conceptually in the concern, in the treatment planning and in the definition of the problem. This does not mean blaming the family, accusing them of having failed one another—they will often enough do that for themselves. It means permitting them to share in the understanding of how the problem arose, and most important, in defining what each of them can do to solve it. Many relatives fear the therapist's blame and his therapeutic efforts to change them beyond their own recognition, so this must be a gentle process.

Third is the therapist's *focus on the current situation* as he overcomes the back drag of emergency, which tends to gravitate to past conflict, often only symbolically relevant to the systems crisis. The therapist was not called in the middle of the night to discuss what was wrong with someone's past history. As the focus is kept on the sequence of events leading up to the request for help, a working definition of the current crisis is achieved. This definition may be incomplete, inaccurate, or still in controversy at the end of the initial interview, and may require subsequent changes. Still, having a working definition upon which all can focus stops much of the destructiveness and diffusion of the emergency and the disruption and disorganization of the crisis.

Fourth, there must be some *relief of the anxiety and disabling symptoms*. This is accomplished to some extent by the emergency response, the involvement of other family members, and the definition of the problem. Relief of tension is also enhanced by the therapist's manner and attitude and by various characteristics of the setting. Medication is invaluable in dealing with psychotic patients and is useful for many neurotic patients and family members.

Fifth, as the definition of the problem proceeds, one or more direct, associated, often simple, solutions begin to become apparent. Each involved family member may become aware of certain *changes he can make in his activity or attitude* to assist in solving the problem. Tasks may be assigned to symbolize these changes and to symbolize transcendance of the crisis state.

Sixth is *negotiation of resistance to change* and conflict over who will change, how, and to what degree. This is, in essence, psychotherapy. It may take a variety of forms, although, hopefully, the particular style of psychotherapy is appropriate for the family's needs rather than just for the therapist's. This phase of crisis therapy may be passed over swiftly or may take a lifetime. It usually is most prominent after the initial interview, when the tasks that would solve the crisis have not been performed and the resistances to performing them are presented. Psychotherapy with a defined problem and, therefore, a defined direction of change is a more specific "treatment" than the vaguely directed, diffuse "growth therapy" that is so common.

The seventh step, *termination,* is really part of the first phase. Termination should be begun initially as a clearly stated limitation of availability and involvement.

Defining the Problem

These seven phases are useful and have proved their value in structuring crisis intervention in several settings. The central and crucial step is the definition of the family problem. Often, the best guide to this is the identification of the crisis-producing stress.

Classification of Crisis-producing Stresses

Various attempts have been made to quantitate stress, but all are unsatisfactory because the degree of stress depends so heavily on the characteristics of the family.

Each family has its own special boundaries, its usual patterns of functioning, its goals, its stock of unresolved conflicts. In addition, each family maintains a certain acceptable level of *tension,* usually varying from day to day. At best, the level may be low enough to permit the members to take off their girdles around one another, but high enough to keep the members "anxious" to please one another. At worst, the tension may be so low, the members feel no responsibility toward one another, or so high, the members are constantly on the verge of homicide or divorce.

"Death of a spouse" is usually considered the most severe stress, yet in some marriages this is a joyous event. Whether "visit from mother-in-law," "fist fight with neighbors," or "Christmas" is a greater stress varies from family to family. Nonetheless, the stress has certain characteristics and it must be identified and described along certain dimensions before it can be handled. Some of these dimensions are:

Overt–covert. If a stress is apparent to everyone involved, it will be stressful in a different way from the stress that is apparent only to a member or segment of the family. Open infidelity is a different problem from secret infidelity; secrets in a family create strangely skewed relationships. If a secret must be maintained at all costs, a stress related to the secret cannot be handled openly, or even defined openly as a stress.

Temporary–permanent. In knowing how to react to a stress, it is important to know the duration of its operation. When the mother-in-law arrives, it helps to know whether she'll be there overnight or forever. When a man is impotent or a woman nonorgastic, it is important to know whether this will be a permanent state or a temporary one.

Habitual–unique. If a stress is temporary, it helps to know if it will return or not. If a son fails a subject in school, is he an academic failure? If a daughter has sex with her boyfriend, is she a loose woman? If a wife neglects the dishes one night, is she a slob? If a man gets drunk, is he a drunk? How often must a stress be repeated before it achieves the definition of habitual? Many family arguments concern this point.

Situational–structural. Does the stress arise from the operations of the family, or did the family experience a bit of bad luck? If a teenage girl is caught in bed with her boyfriend, is it defined as "we live in a society which is sexually stimulating" or "where did we fail?" or "she's doing it to hurt her poor mother who has slaved for her"? If she becomes pregnant, is the definition "she's no good," "he's no good," or "this is a bad situation"? If she becomes pregnant a second time, is it defined as "she has bad luck" or "perhaps there's something she or we are doing wrong"?

Resolving the Crisis

The stress throws the family into crisis. The crisis state is characterized by disruption of the usual patterns, by interruption and reevaluation of the family's goals, its cherished values, its definition of itself, and often by a loosening of its boundaries. With this there may be a revival of the old unresolved issues and an increase in tension between the members. The comfortable repertoire of roles and rules no longer serves.

The crisis may be resolved by defining the stress and making the appropriate changes in patterns or goals. This unfortunately sounds easier than it is for many families.

Attempted solutions often are excessive, or inappropriate, and may be further sources of stress. The husband may change jobs or give up golf; the wife may kill herself or neglect the housework; the daughter may run away, and the son may beat up his father, or the family may change churches, or dissolve, or leave town, or do nothing, ignoring the structural problem. The stress is often difficult to define since the precipitating issue frequently is not contained in the presenting complaint. People rarely come to the crisis therapist saying, "We're a family in crisis," although someone may say, "I've been nervous since my in-laws visited us," "There's no point in living since my wife left me," "She resents us so much that we can't control her," or even in one case, "He tries to kill himself every time his father gets drunk, but I'm afraid we'll have no social life at all if we quit drinking."

Sometimes complaints imply efforts to solve a crisis, as "Help me adjust to a family that doesn't love me" or "If I were only stronger maybe I could hold the family together." More often, the definition implies a faulty resolution of a recent crisis, as "She's gone crazy again. She's schizophrenic you know," "He's so disturbed, he's even blaming me," "I'm just rundown," or "I know you'll blame my parents, but it's just me. I've never been any good. They'll tell you that."

Often, there is an attempt to *ignore the stress* and proceed as if the usual patterns and goals could still operate. After a financial loss, a family might continue the old spending patterns rather than face the need to rebudget. A child, grown to adolescence, may still be treated as an asexual child. The knowledge of infidelity, or even incest, may be denied as the family continues as it always has. In these cases, the stress, if defined at all, is seen as covert, temporary or unique, and situational, which may not be so at all.

There may be an attempt to resolve the crisis by various forms of *over-reaction.* A potentially minor stress may be seen as not only overt, but public news, permanent or habitual, and highly structural. For resolution, the entire system may be drastically redefined, the membership may be changed and the family disrupted. Under these circumstances: "we'll get a divorce," "we'll disown you," or "we'll dedicate ourselves to God."

A third kind of faulty resolution is *to place full responsibility on one individual.* He may escape by going home to Mother or running away from home or developing an incapacitating symptom or going to a mental hospital. He may become the family scapegoat, blamed increasingly for the family's problems, a role not very conducive to continued good functioning. He may become the family doctor, given the responsibility of solving the family's problems, a role which, if performed successfully, may prepare him for a later career in one of the helping professions, but which, if performed badly, may lead him to need help.

Each faulty resolution, of course, then becomes a new stress and begins the process anew. In time, after a series of faulty resolutions, it may be difficult to determine the initial stress. The family may be in a state of constant upset.

Fortunately, the crisis state involves one feature that provides the therapist with an opportunity he does not have at other times, i.e., the loosening of boundaries permits him to enter the family. Unfortunately there is a trap set by the crisis state, i.e., the revival of past conflicts may barrage him with interesting but irrelevant issues, deflecting him from the current crisis.

With this understanding of the crisis process, the treatment of crisis and its associated emergency can be made far less chaotic than it usually appears. It does require some effort on the therapist's part to keep the therapeutic work problem-oriented rather than solution-oriented, i.e., to let the solution arise from the problems being treated, rather than to work on the problems he likes to solve. Too often, the therapist has his own solution and is in search of a problem. He deflects attention from the current crisis to some other problem ripe for solving, which, however real, is also peripheral.

A distinction should be made between "treatment," the pointed effort to solve a specific problem, and "therapy," the nonspecific process of improving people's mental health and adaptability and helping them to grow. It is fine to combine the two, but treatment should not be sacrificed to "therapy" during a crisis.

Defining the Crisis

An example of the process of defining the crisis: Mr. Clay called my private office for an emergency appointment for his 18-yr-old daughter, Carol. He had been referred by another psychiatrist who specialized in adolescent problems but was unable to see her for several weeks. Mr. Clay revealed that Carol had run away from home and been on drugs, had now returned, and was threatening to leave again. I explained that I preferred to see the family, at least initially, but could not do so for 5 days. Carol agreed to stay home until the appointment. With this immediate response, the situation cooled somewhat. Meanwhile, I made myself available for any emergency.

The day prior to the scheduled appointment, Mrs. Clay called to cancel the appointment. She had decided to admit herself to a hospital. Hysterically, she said that her husband and daughter were allied against her, blaming her for all the problems. She feared she would kill herself or them. I asked her to drop by the office for a one-day supply of a minor tranquilizer and told her, if necessary, to spend the night at a friend's house. On the day of the appointment, Carol and her father arrived first, Mrs. Clay was late, coming from an older daughter's house, where she'd had her first good night's sleep in weeks after taking the pills.

Each of the three saw the situation differently. Carol was a high school graduate, presently employed at a job she liked. She had no interest in going to college, although her four older siblings had all attended college, while living at home. She had moved out of the family home after her graduation from high school and had lived with a young married couple. This created so much opposition from both parents that she had ceased contact with them for several weeks, until they notified her at work of her grandmother's imminent death 6 wk before. She admitted to occasional use of alcohol and marijuana, no harder drugs. She was now living at home under protest to pacify her parents. She saw both parents as over-protective and saw her father as trying to keep her home to pacify her mother, who was still mourning the grandmother.

Mr. Clay saw Carol as breaking the family tradition of children who had lived at home even after their own marriages. He did not approve of Carol's job or life style and blamed his wife for making it intolerable for Carol at home.

Mrs. Clay saw Carol and Mr. Clay as allied against her. She was less concerned with where Carol lived than she was with what her own life would be like in the big house alone with her husband and an older son who was rarely home and no longer needed her. She felt that no one needed or cared about her since the death of her invalid mother, whom she had nursed full-time for 5 yr.

The history-taking was interrupted by repeated accusations of past conflicts, Mrs. Clay accusing Mr. Clay and Carol of "never" having cared sufficiently about the grandmother or about her, Mr. Clay accusing his wife of "always" being too fussy with the children and thereby running them off, and Carol accusing both parents of "always" treating her as a child. Review of the history confirmed that the family had functioned to everyone's satisfaction prior to the grandmother's illness, at which point Mrs. Clay quit her cherished job to nurse her mother, and began to give less attention to the rest of the family. The family

adjusted to this change without major upset, as Mr. Clay devoted more attention to the children and less to his wife. The current crisis began when the
grandmother's health plummeted. The immediate response to this crisis was to
try to bring Carol home. Carol's response was to try to detach herself further,
although she finally agreed to come home when her grandmother was dying.
Neither Mr. nor Mrs. Clay seemed able to be close to the other, having always
had children and mothers to keep them apart. The obvious solution to the
grandmother's death was for the Clays to learn to live as a twosome. This
degree of change terrified both, so Mr. Clay brought Carol in as a buffer.

The apparent stress, the grandmother's death, was overt, permanent, unique,
and situational, but the real stress for the Clays was the habitual, structural,
and covert conflict of how to buffer themselves against closeness to one another, always more of a problem for Mr. Clay than for his wife. The first definition of the crisis, used by both parents, was an effort to scapegoat Carol. By
declaring Carol a juvenile, unstable, drug-using runaway, they could get her
home as a buffer. Carol was willing to come home temporarily to help her
mother through her mourning, but 6 wk later the arrangement seemed too permanent for her. The next definition attempted was Mr. Clay's: "You'll have to
stay home because your mother's gone crazy." Mrs. Clay acted out the part,
but it infuriated her, so she moved out, hysterically pin-pointing the real problem, that Mr. Clay was allied with Carol to prevent the closeness with him she
feared but wanted.

In the 2-hr interview, the focus had shifted from the nominal patient, Carol,
to the symptomatic member, Mrs. Clay, to the member who was resisting a
crisis-resolving change, Mr. Clay. A definition of the problem was achieved:
how to separate the issue of Carol's independence from the process of reestab-
lishing closeness between husband and wife now that they were sitting on an
empty nest.

Mrs. Clay's depression was deemed sufficiently serious to prescribe anti-
depressants. She agreed to return home. Carol agreed to stay home for 2 wk
more and to keep her parents involved in her plans for living away from home.
The greatest responsibility for change fell on Mr. Clay who was expected by
Carol to reevaluate his goal of keeping his children at home, and was expected
by Mrs. Clay to go through another courtship with her. Mrs. Clay could return
to work to make her less totally frightening to her obsessive spouse and less
totally dependent upon him. Over a few weeks, the various resistances to these
proposed specific changes were examined and the process of treatment focused
on the fears of marital closeness between Mr. and Mrs. Clay. Much attention
was given to Mr. Clay's unusual background (he had been raised by deaf
mutes), which made him distrust verbal communication of the sort demanded
by his wife. As they became closer to one another, Carol could remain involved
with them without fear of being engulfed, and, finally, even the past conflicts
could be worked through.

The process of defining this crisis was started by proposing a series of faulty
solutions, designed to skirt the real issue. Two of these were requests for some
sort of psychiatric intervention, the request for treatment for Carol for her drug
abuse, and the request for hospitalization of Mrs. Clay. Once these were both

denied, it became possible to define and then treat the real crisis triggered by the grandmother's death.

Postscript

Family relationships are close and interdependent: Anything affecting one individual affects his family and vice versa. A change in an individual, whether that change is abrupt and accidental or a necessary and anticipated development in the life history of the individual, necessarily produces changes in other family members, and those changes produce further changes. It may even be difficult at times to recall which family member made the first change, if we can even conceive of a first change in a family, which is constantly dealing with change.

The therapist in his attempts to deal with psychiatric breakdown must have a *focused* sense of these complexities, which allows him to be aware of them, yet to patiently adhere to the task of defining the precipitating stress and the systems changes it has produced. Above all, he must recognize his own part in the process and his limitations. In this spirit, we may close with the story, undoubtedly apocryphal, that has been told of five famous family therapists who appeared successively for teaching sessions at a family therapy institute. Each was a terrible prima donna and wanted this opportunity to show himself off at his most splendid. Each requested just the sort of family that would make him look most impressive for the students, but a wise and spiteful genie mixed up the families so that each prima donna interviewed a family precisely opposite in character from the one requested. The therapist who specialized in playing grandfather to Jewish triads was given a tribe of Apaches. The therapist who was at his best going crazy in front of disorganized families and demanding that they treat him by organizing, was given a Jewish triad in search of a grandfather. The therapist who cooled off families in crisis by ignoring overt pathology and focusing on cleaning kitchen sinks was given two normal couples who had never met. The therapist who used love and activity to loosen up non-communicative obsessives was given a family in homicidal, suicidal, psychotic chaos over current conflicts. The therapist who taught fathers to be dominant, while herding families from room to room, was given one room, a dominant father, and a competing male co-therapist. The students learned that there is no magic and there are no magicians, nor is there one way to treat everybody.

REFERENCES

1. Flomenhaft K, Kaplan DM, Langsley DG: Avoiding psychiatric hospitalization. Soc Work October 1969, pp 38–45

2. Haley J, Hoffman L: Cleaning house: An interview with Frank Pittman, III, Kalman Flomenhaft, and Carol DeYoung, in Haley J, Hoffman L (eds): Techniques of Family Therapy. New York, Basic Books, 1967, pp 361–471

3. Kaplan DM: A concept of acute situational disorders. Soc Work 7:15–23, 1962

4. Kritzer H, Pittman FS III: Overnight psychiatric care in a general hospital emergency room. Hosp Community Psychiatry 19:21–24, 1968

5. Langsley DG, Fairbairn RH, DeYoung CD: Adolescence and family crises. Can Psychiatr Assoc J 13:125–133, 1968

6. Langsley DG, Kaplan DM, Pittman FS III, et al: The Treatment of Families in Crisis. New York, Grune & Stratton, 1968

7. Langsley DG, Pittman FS III, Machotka

P, et al: Family crisis therapy—results and implication. Fam Process 7:145–158, 1968

8. Langsley DG, Pittman FS III, Swank GE: Family crises in schizophrenics and other mental patients. J Nerv Ment Dis 149:270–276, 1969

9. Machotka P, Pittman FS III, Flomenhaft K: Incest as a family affair. Fam Process 6:98–116, 1967

10. Pittman FS III: A comprehensive emergency service as an alternative to hospitalization, in McGee RK (ed): Planning Emergency Treatment Services for Comprehensive Community Mental Health Centers, Conference Proceedings. Gainesville, Fla, University of Florida, 1967, pp 33–42

11. Pittman FS III, DeYoung CD, Flomenhaft K, et al: Crisis family therapy, in Masserman JH (ed): Current Psychiatric Therapies, vol 6. New York, Grune & Stratton, 1966, pp 187–196

12. Pittman FS III, Flomenhaft K: Treating the doll's house family. Fam Process 9:143–155, 1970

13. Pittman FS III, Langsley DG, Kaplan DM, et al: Family therapy as an alternative to psychiatric hospitalization, in Psychiatric Research Report 20. Washington, DC, American Psychiatric Association, 1966

14. Pittman FS III, Langsley DG, Flomenhaft K, et al: Therapy techniques of the family treatment unit, in Haley J (ed): Changing Families, A Family Therapy Reader. New York, Grune & Stratton, 1971

Problems of the Beginning Family Therapist

Augustus Y. Napier, Ph.D. and Carl Whitaker, M.D.

W HETHER he is a young student or a seasoned individual therapist who has changed orientation, the person who works at becoming a family therapist must be credited with a certain amount of courage. The field is itself young, the way uncertain, and families and their stresses are powerful. While the authors do not like to think of family psychotherapy as schematized and rigidly ordered (at its best it should be spontaneous and creative), it would be helpful to have at least a crude map for the journey. Many therapists are currently and gradually establishing such a map, often enough from stumbling into briar patches and sloughs of despond. This is a valid way to learn, but painful; and sometimes we learn at the expense of families. This paper represents a documentation of such learning. Somewhat unfairly, it deals primarily with problems or "errors" and does not prescribe a definite pattern for the therapist, although some of the problem areas point toward alternative strategies. The authors' most intimate experience with these problems has been through their own mistakes, although they have also gained perspective from their seminars for young students of family therapy. It is also somewhat unfair to assume that only beginning therapists encounter these problems. To some extent they cause us all difficulty.

Family therapy is of course a new field in which several different conceptual worlds, each with its own sense of correctness and morality, contend. The authors can only state their own conceptual viewpoint, one that necessarily involves personal values, in order that the reader can establish our general position on the larger map. The basic ingredient in the family therapy used as a model here is the experience of *encounter*, the electricity of the face-to-face moment. In our practice, therapy begins by the therapists' setting a structure within which the encounter can take place, usually including the whole nuclear family and *two therapists*, but often including extended family members and involved "outsiders." The encounter has three principal dimensions. Initially, the most charged encounter takes place between family members; the co-therapists are professional and attempt to catalyze that opening-up process. As the family comes to trust the co-therapists, the intensity of that family confrontation deepens. Therapy moves from reality struggles to symbolic struggles to personal struggles; and finally, hopefully, to warmly personal spontaneity. This does not occur, however, without the second area of encounter, the model provided by the co-therapists' interaction with each other; the co-therapeutic relationship is a visible alternative way of relating, and it provides support for each therapist's interaction with the family. Yet, the most crucial encounter is built upon the increasing personal involvement of each family member and each therapist in the therapy process itself. The critical moments in the therapy are

Reprint requests should be addressed to Augustus Y. Napier, Ph.D., Wisconsin Children's Treatment Center, 3418 Harper Road, Madison, Wisc. 53704.

in the dialogue between one therapist and one family member. These encounters lead to the development of a "culture of caring" in the family–therapist group.

The authors believe that the therapist's person, and his search for growth, is an essential ingredient in family therapy. Another assumption concerns the level of that involvement: The intuitive and feeling response is more important than rational understanding. Psychotherapy is basically seen as a spontaneous human process that is facilitated by professional involvement but cannot be programmed. It can, however, be inhibited; and this paper deals primarily with conditions that limit the therapeutic group's creativity and effectiveness.

Lack of Leadership

The need for leadership is especially acute in a family where crisis threatens both its structure and its function. Often a member is about to be expelled, or the family is failing to function as a unit. In dealing with these high-stress situations, the therapist should be in control of the therapy hour and should set certain conditions which, in his professional judgment, maximize the chances for success. Families usually test the therapist's strength, and they often do so around the issue of structure. They attempt to decrease their anxiety by trying to set the structure; for example, by trying to tell the therapist who should attend the interview. This testing phase is seen as a "battle for structure," and the therapist must win this struggle in order to earn the family's trust in his strength. Many family therapists insist on the whole family being present before beginning treatment, realizing that withholding treatment is one of the few real points of leverage the therapist has, and believing that effective treatment is greatly enhanced when the whole patient (the family) is present. But many therapists prefer other arrangements: Murray Bowen,[2] for example, prefers to work with the married couple. Whatever the therapist's convictions, he should surely and decisively approach the family's anxiety about structure. He should lead rather than follow the family's decision about membership at the session. Many inexperienced therapists are reluctant to challenge the family and simply accept whoever the family brings to the session. The family quickly senses this indecisiveness and intuitively protects its integrity by participating only half-heartedly in sessions, reducing stress by omitting key members. The experienced therapist is more authoritative: He requires to be present family members he feels he needs; he brings in a co-therapist, or recording aids, without permission; he asks members to arrange their seating in a certain way—he moves with confidence. In short, he provides ropes (structure) for the boxing ring, believing that only within such a firm structure can intense conflict be successfully negotiated. Some provision is necessary to insure that the attacked person returns to work it out.

Failure to Include Extended Family

Many treatment efforts fail because important people are absent from the sessions. While the need for all nuclear family members to be present has been well documented in the literature, the authors are increasingly convinced that the family of *origin* often undermines family therapy aimed at the family of *procreation.* The experience of Speck[7] and his associates indicates that the process of assembling a kin and social network prior to the first session is an important part of therapy, and network therapists insist on involvement of the extended family. In our haste to be helpful, we probably often fail to do adequate preparation for the first interview—finding out who is involved and should be part of the therapeutic effort. Once therapy has begun, it seems much more difficult to involve members of the system who perceive themselves as outsiders to the therapeutic group. The therapists may not be aware of the need for certain individuals until an impasse develops in mid-phase—for example, the point where an individuation attempt by the marital pair fails because of their fear of breaking with their parents. It seems far preferable to anticipate such an impasse by enlisting the participation of the extended family early in treatment. Similar considerations apply to other therapists involved with the family. The authors prefer to begin with a large first meeting that includes all of the available extended family, previous or concurrent therapists, and "involved" outsiders. Subsets of this initial group are asked to return to therapy as need for them arises.

Over-eagerness to Help

A certain kind of impasse results when the therapists dominate the interaction by comment and interpretation. Characteristically, the family speaks a few sentences to each other, or speaks to one of the therapists about a family member, and the therapists are off—advising, commenting, questioning, interpreting, working. Soon the family falls silent and the therapists probe again to create more activity. A great deal of talk about life ensues, but little of any affective significance occurs and the family and therapists leave depressed. If the therapists work hard enough and the family is stoic, this kind of stalemate can persist for months. This dilemma usually derives from the family's anxiety about such encounter. Furthermore, the therapists may have a distorted view of what they can and cannot provide: They attempt to provide motivation for change.

There are several reasons for the therapists' insisting quite early in the therapy process that the family members talk *to each other* about their problems and that they actively strive with each other to solve them: (1) They may be able to resolve the problems quickly in this way, using the support of the therapists. to intensify encounter that previously has been inhibited; (2) they expose their system to the therapists, giving them "real" and affectively charged material rather than stale description; (3) they begin to take initiative and control of their lives and may discover excitedly that *they* can change themselves; and (4) they may experience increased despair at their own self-defeating pressure tactics and thus convincingly lay the groundwork for the entry of the therapists at a significant level.

Many young therapists are aware of the need to get the family to interact, but are unaware of how they subtly undermine this process. Often they become anxious and active at precisely the moment when something begins to happen in the family. The therapist may also equate quantity of verbalization with quality of therapy, and feel guilty if the family is not talking enough. The therapist may be anxious or depressed and may need to continue to talk in order to conceal his own affect. He may fear aloneness and be reluctant to "just sit" while the family works, fantasizing himself as symbolically cast out of the family; fear of aloneness is particularly poignant for the therapist without a co-therapist.

Worst of all, the therapist may feel he must supply motivation for change. All families, and all individuals, seem to both wish for, and fear, change; while the therapist may help the family struggle with this ambivalence, he probably cannot resolve it for them. He cannot supply motivation and should be some-what humble about this reality. Indeed, his *trying* to supply initiative may make it less likely that the family discovers their own motivation for change. Perhaps the therapist finds himself in this dilemma because he accuses himself of being inadequate and ungiving: "If only I had bigger breasts." He works hard to overcome his perceived inadequacy when in reality the therapeutic effort *is* dependent on the family's contribution. A firm, persistent, gentle insistence—"Go ahead, try struggling with each other; I think you can do it!"—may provide the needed start. In some instances, the therapist may need to refuse to supply any push, simply waiting while the family struggles to find its own resources.

One way of conceptualizing the balance of initiative in therapy is as follows. The therapist contributes a good deal of himself in the first interview or two, in part to give the family some idea of what he is like and what he can contribute. Then he makes demands for the family to contribute initiative in exposing and struggling with their problems in the therapy hour. Gradually a reciprocal agreement is established in which each side contributes to each interview.

Extra-therapeutic Communications

Many families attempt to reduce tension by communicating with the therapists outside the session, and beginning therapists are particularly susceptible to such ploys. The family may also have their own "therapeutic encounters" outside the session, cheating the therapy hour of needed affect. Persuading the family to concentrate their stressful interactions, their arguments, their accusations in the interviews is difficult, but it seems the only way to integrate the trends that pull the family in different directions. The therapist can certainly ask the family member who calls to "save it for the session" without being rejecting. And he can ask the family to postpone its arguments until the therapy session. "Centering" the effort on the therapy hour is probably facilitated if the therapists reciprocate, doing the majority of their talking about the family in front of the family. If the therapists joke and complain about the family privately, their involvement with the family is decreased and valuable affect about the family is dissipated.

Treating the Scapegoat

While recent research by Postner et al.[5] indicates that it may be essential to deal thoroughly with the "identified patient's" dynamics in the process of treatment, it seems to be a tactical error to focus on this person *initially*. So doing essentially agrees with the family's definition of their problem, and reinforces the scapegoating process by enlisting the family's help in treating the "patient." Many therapists who profess interest in the family system nevertheless proceed to treat the individual within a family therapy structure. The writers prefer to attack the "patient" myth in the first interview and to democratize the stress by implicating the whole family in its patterns. It is usually possible to expose the marital conflict, the sibling patterns, and the overall tone of stress and despair in the family during the first interview. The scapegoat is usually delighted to be ignored or slighted for the time being. Of course once therapy is under way, this individual's problems should be dealt with, but preferably out of the individual's initiative and in their own good time.

The Previous Therapist

It is easy for family therapists to ignore previous therapists, assuming the family approach allows everyone to "start over." The family therapist's ignorance of the effects of previous therapy can seriously hamper the work. The most damaging case is when a therapist moves from individual therapy with one family member to treating the family and assumes that he does not, at least in part, see the family through this person's eyes. At the very least, the family deserves one therapist who can relate to the whole group without bias, if not a new and unbiased team.

Another common dilemma involves a family in which one marital partner has had extensive individual therapy and the other little or none. Often the naïve member is the husband, and often he feels threatened by therapy and is covertly enraged at therapists in general. If strong efforts are not made to equalize this perceived imbalance in experience, the naïve member may withdraw the family from treatment. In many such cases, one of the family therapists should probably have a few individual sessions with the naïve spouse, or the team should encourage the family to work on their feelings about previous treatment.

Complex patterns can arise out of previous therapy. One family had previous family therapy in which the mother was found to be the "sick one" and the therapists reputedly encouraged the children to act out against the parents. The new family therapists were mystified and offended by mother's defensiveness until they learned of its origin. They were systematically tempted into several patterns—"I knew you would see my husband as victimized—they did too" —and then told how stupid they were. Not until they worked through their negative feeling about previous treatment did the family begin to move.

Difficulties in Teaming

If a co-therapist team treats the family, as the writers feel they should in view of the family's enormous power, difficulties in maintaining cooperation between the therapists are extremely common. The most serious difficulty results from a basic disrespect of the therapists for each other, a disrespect that results in covert warfare between them. Young male co-therapists are often overly competitive and simply shout down the family in an effort to impress each other. Therapists with different conceptual orientations also have difficulty, especially if the conceptual orientations represent very different personal value constellations, such as authoritarian versus laissez-faire approaches. A certain amount of complementarity between the therapists seems helpful, however, since unde-detected countertransference often stems from co-therapists having similar personalities or similar family histories. Intellectual disagreement seems gen-erally less a problem than personality conflict.

In the authors' opinion the only remedy for conflict between therapists is to make the covert disagreement overt, preferably before the family where its resolution can provide a model for them. Certainly, the family is aware of such divergence in the team. If the feeling is intense and involves personal issues, a consultant is probably necessary to help resolve the differences. Some dis-agreement is probably minimized if each therapist can feel secure enough to let the other "do his thing" and discover, in the process of trying, how much he needs a compatriot. The beginning family therapist should probably see at least one family alone (but observed by a co-worker) so that he has some ground in which to express his creativity with minimal interference.

Side-taking

Most family therapists rationally see the advantage of not taking sides with one individual, particularly early in therapy; but in practice it is extremely difficult to do. At every turn there is opportunity to be drawn into partisanship, particularly in the marital struggle or the generation war. Bowen[1] has written extensively about the need for the therapist to "detriangle" the family's efforts to entangle him and to remain neutral and objective. While this seems an ad-mirable goal in the early stages of treatment, it seems limiting if pursued throughout. The therapist's active involvement need not be damaging if it de-velops gradually out of a sense of caring about the family's fate, if it is not locked into one person's view, and if it is tempered by the perspective of the co-therapist. But early and partisan over-involvement of a therapist is a common problem, causing the family to doubt the therapist's fairness and judgment. Taking sides is often perceived as an invasion and reacted to defensively.

The most difficult problem occurs when the therapist meets one marital part-ner, if only for a few sessions, and if only to discuss issues like child manage-ment. The therapist's view of the family is subtly colored by this individual con-tact, and the other spouse's *perception* of this bias is amplified many-fold. As noted above, this biasing can be deliberate, but therapists should be aware of its effect.

Countertransference in the therapists, in combination with blaming patterns in the family, accounts for much early side-taking. The therapist is drawn into a morass of moral politics. In one team, both male co-therapists were from homes where the mother was overtly powerful, the father overtly weak. Their work with a family with a similar pattern went poorly until they both realized they sided with "downtrodden" father but allowed mother to dominate the hour. When they realized their joint vulnerability to this situation, they were able to deal more effectively with the family dilemma. Countertransference is a particularly serious problem for young family therapists, since they are drawn into an active struggle involving a powerful group. Often the young therapist feels like a child of the family he is treating. The family therapist's current marital problems are particularly influential, since they are likely to be more emotionally charged than the patterns out of his family of origin and can easily find their way into his perception of the patient family. In fact, *transference in the therapist* might be a preferable term, since he responds primarily to the pattern of the family's involvement with each other rather than to their involvement with him. Perhaps the most serious problem in family therapy, the therapist's transference, can also be a powerful stimulus to his personal growth.

One of the more subtle forms of side-taking results from the therapist's use of our currently inadequate conceptual framework, particularly those ideas that attribute cause and effect. This is a thinly disguised version of the good and evil debate, evil being "cause" and good being the victimized "effect." A typical example is the therapist's believing "he dominates her." Jackson's[3] use of the *quid pro quo* argument offers some relief from this gross over-simplification, asserting that such a pattern develops out of a mutual and implicit agreement in which each party derives benefits. An even more sophisticated conceptualization looks beneath overt behavior, positing that the overtly submissive wife is the equal in power of her loud mate but is simply more covert in her expression.

A similar dichotomization can attribute health to some family members, illness to others; looking beneath overt behavior often reveals similar levels of stress in all family members, stress which is simply expressed in diverse ways, including somatically. The beginning therapist is excessively impressed by overt patterns, and he tends to grasp familiar but inadequate concepts of causality, or health and illness, which involve him in a kind of moralistic side-taking. Furthermore, he tends to think dyadically rather than in larger configurational patterns. In part, this over-simplification represents cultural atavism, but it can also represent an attempt to structure a bewildering new environment. We all struggle with the lack of adequate conceptual tools in the face of family complexity.

Pseudo-mutual Neutrality

Many families enter therapy guarded and "pseudo-mutual."[9] They refuse to challenge each other overtly. The therapist's parallel neutrality—coolly reflective, rational, finding support for every attacked person, finding a counter-blame for every blame—can perpetuate the family's facade. It is a difficult task for the therapist to break the facade by momentarily attacking one spouse or one child without jeopardizing his availability to the whole family. Yet unless he challenges the facade, everyone may die of boredom. Perhaps the most effective way is to listen for micro-challenges in the family itself and to amplify them: "He *is* a nag, isn't he." But the therapist must be a broken-field runner, ready to move from the other person's vantage point when necessary, not firmly identified with one position. This kind of floating, temporary advocacy is difficult to achieve and demands a certain amount of benign uninvolvement in the therapist at the outset of treatment. At times, sympathetic but temporary response to one family member, rather than attack on someone, will be enough to disrupt the equilibrium. Other family members become jealous and breech the family appearance of conformity to gain the therapist's attention.

Over-identification With the Family

If transference involves the therapist in family structure, the therapist's dependency can over-involve him in the family's style and tone of interaction. A depressed family causes both therapists to relate seriously and sadly. A hostile family causes the therapists to relate in an attacking manner. Perhaps the most serious problem is the therapist who becomes anxious in the face of the family's anxiety, a situation that may make all his comments seem accusatory and blaming. Every remark finds something negative in the family, and the family's defensiveness produces even more negative comment. This cycle is rooted in projected self-blame in both family and therapists, and it can quickly lead to early termination.

It is very difficult for the beginning therapist to "feel" where the family is affectively, to be empathic, yet to be able to relate at times on a different affective level—to respond casually or humorously, for example, to an explosively tense argument. When he does respond on a different affective level, he tends to be defending against the family's affect because it threatens him, and his alternative affect is often perceived as rejecting or mocking. Being able to slip in and out of the family's affect requires a hard-earned agility and considerable maturity. A co-therapist's support makes learning this process much easier.

Failure to Involve the Entire Family

Having the family all in the room does not accomplish engaging them all in therapy. Family therapy seems to really begin to move when everyone in the family can participate affectively in the interview; they need to feel involved in the experience, even if they are not verbal. Some family members hang back out of the family's agreement to reduce stress in this way, but the therapist's transference may also be a factor. The first author unwittingly ignored a teenage girl in one family for nearly a year until the family reported she was suicidal. He realized later that he had been embarrassed at his fondness for her since she reminded him of his sister; he had unintentionally scapegoated her by refusing even to look directly at her. When she finally joined the family debate and began to interact openly with the therapists, everyone seemed to breathe a sigh of relief and the work proceeded rapidly. The therapist need not push silent members to participate, but he should make it clear that he is available to them. Much of this openness can be communicated nonverbally, or through casual comment.

Prestructuring

If one assumes that encounter, and particularly the quality of that encounter, determines the outcome of psychotherapy, then attempting to prestructure or prepare for the therapy session can be seen as seriously inhibiting the power of that encounter. The therapists may try to plan what will happen—to get the parents to fight, to get the father to be more assertive, to get the child to talk. The results of this pressure are self-consciousness in the therapist, and suspiciousness and resistance in the family. However painful life may be for them, the family wonders nevertheless what the therapists are doing to the family group they depend on. They feel what Thomas Malone[4] has called "the tyranny of compulsion," a tyranny against which they rebel. The usual outcome is a firm and somewhat angry stasis. But even if the planning and pushing by the therapists is open and explained, the session tends to be low-key, businesslike, and impersonal. The electricity of personal encounter is missing, the tricky tension of the here-and-now. If one trusts the creativity of the moment and waits for important and meaningful events to occur spontaneously, it is far more likely that the events and feelings will have the badly needed power of immediacy.

The therapist's constant interference with a naturally developing group process may derive from his conviction that he must supply explicit direction and supervision. In effect, he becomes a nag. A more powerful strategy seems to be to attempt to give the family two perspectives: (1) a poignant awareness of their *present state* including its patterning, its affective tone, and some of its origins; and to give them (2) a different model for interaction through the co-therapists' relationship with each other and through the therapists' response to the family. But it is best to let the family move selectively, at its own speed and volition, from where they are to where they perceive the therapists to be, not constantly pushing them to accept the therapists' world. If it is useful or appealing to the family, they will move toward this new model.

Stereotyped Focus

However open the therapist may be to the family's immediate affect, the family still turns to the therapist for cues as to how they should behave within the therapy hour, and to some extent every therapist supplies those cues. Some therapists will be interested in the individual's past, some in the married couple's moment-to-moment communications, some in structural dynamics, some in the various individuals' feelings. Usually the family tries to conform to these mostly inexplicit expectations. A common failing of therapists is to become too loyal to one conceptual viewpoint and to try too hard to *teach* it as if it somehow represented an "answer" to the family's problems. Teaching is a valuable thing for the family, but it preferably comes after the critical encounter phases of the therapy.

Optimally, the therapist approaches the family with genuine curiosity—open to the rapid to-and-fro of interaction, hoping to learn from it. This openness demands a tolerance for ambiguity and uncertainty in himself, and it means that he will often be mystified. By allowing himself to become confused and mystified, however, the therapist can make new discoveries about this and all families, and the family's perception of "newness" in the therapist's ideas and reactions creates an impact that teaching from a "prelearned" point of reference can never have. The best mental attitude for such casting about seems to be what Reik[6] has described as "free-floating attention," in which the therapist lets his attention drift casually as he listens. In this attitude, the therapist should trust his intuition, attending to his own fleeting responses. Learning to recognize and to share his own covert responses is often difficult for the beginning therapist, since he tends to mistrust them. Often they represent to him his own anxiety, his anger, his guilty sexuality, his personal problems. It is probably not until the therapist has resolved his more pressing life-problems and is fairly comfortable in the interview hour that he can draw freely and spontaneously on his intuitive responses to the family. The therapist's intuitive response to the family may be confusing for them, but this confusion may be a necessary precursor to a new and less stereotyped order in the family.

Some foci seem particularly unproductive, and a tempting one for beginning therapists is to become too concerned with reality issues—whether Johnny quits school, whether mother files for divorce, whether the family takes a vacation trip. Psychotherapy seems necessary, in fact, only because reality issues are invested with symbolic importance (an "overload" of everyday experience that mystifies the family). If the therapist relates to the family largely around reality issues, he tends to miss their symbolic importance. Moreover he is easily drawn into and used in the power struggles in the family.

Some young therapists focus too heavily on content, missing process cues. The process interpretation is perhaps the most powerful, since it relates to an immediate, and difficult to deny, event. But therapists who relate exclusively to the processes of interaction can bring therapy to a standstill because the family becomes self-conscious—"Did you see what you did with your hands when he said that?" The therapist's ability for multiple focus, to perceive events on several levels, and to draw flexibly from these diverse views of the family seems crucial in producing a creative climate.

An important capability of the therapist seems to be his ability to use himself to model openness and self-disclosure by sharing at least part of his own person. The therapist's fantasy, his slip of the tongue, his feelings in response to the family—all these can provide a valuable lesson in openness for the family. The therapist need not burden the family with his life-problems outside the interview, but his moment-to-moment reactivity to the group situation can make a valuable contribution. All too often the therapist focuses demandingly on the family, trying to force a closed and repetitive system to make a "quantum jump" in process without supplying them with a model toward which they can work.

Another unproductive focus seems to center around teaching one person to "hear" another person's communication. This amounts to scolding one person for not being more empathic or understanding. While the lack of understanding and accurate "hearing" in the family may be very real, it usually represents projected self-blame. That is, the husband cannot be more responsive and empathic to his wife because he has similarly rejecting and punitive attitudes toward his own person, and his wife has a similar struggle. Pushing the family to supply a caring and empathy they do not feel quickly leads to their becoming irritated and angry: "I can't feel sorry for him!" What seems to be needed is a response in the therapist to first one then the other family member, which supplies "information" that is really new to the family: i.e., projected self-acceptance. The therapist sees part of himself in the patient and relates warmly to that person out of a loving, instead of a blaming, identification—a kind of response that usually occurs later in therapy, after the therapist has developed a genuine involvement with the family.

Administrative Solutions

It is quite tempting for the beginning therapist to turn to structural or administrative solutions to interpersonal problems. The first author found one family following a distressing pattern: mother would attack father, and he would feebly counterattack; sensing his weakness, daughter would defend father; then mother and daughter would fight for the remainder of the session. In an attempt to change this boring pattern, the author persuaded the team to see the couple alone for several sessions. Mother attacked father with such force that he, deprived of his daughter's support, became panicked and threatened to take the family out of treatment. When the whole family was finally seen again, the children felt alienated from the therapists, who they felt had sided with the older generation. The primary mistake was in the therapist's failure to respect the family's homeostatic needs, in his attempt to legislate change, in his inability to wait patiently, and in his failure to deal personally in a face-to-face manner with the whole family. Fortunately, a consultation enabled the team to resolve some of these issues. The beginning therapist is plagued with impatience, and with the drive to *do* something. Simply *being* with the family while they struggle is difficult for the anxious beginner, but it often is necessary. Of course the therapist need not be really passive—he can feel and think and react and thus catalyze change in the family without trying to supply action itself.

Fear of Involvement

A common initial problem for the beginning therapist is to become overly involved with the family. In addition to implicating him in family struggles, this interpsychic involvement may cause him to feign a concern and caring he does not really feel for the family. He is then either rebuffed by the family, or feels panicked about his over-involvement and quickly withdraws, becoming excessively distant and cool.

The reverse of this sequence is more appropriate: cool but considerate competence in the beginning, with increasing personal involvement as the relationship develops and as the family changes. The therapist's involvement is perhaps the most critical element in psychotherapy, critical in its timing, its quality, and its intensity. Some kind of involvement is appropriate at all stages, but a caring involvement seems essential in the later stages of therapy.

A thorough discussion of the stages of experiential family therapy is beyond the scope of his paper. A brief view of several stages should provide a perspective on the therapist's degree of emotional involvement in the treatment process. During the first stage, the therapist is quite assertive, setting a firm structure, getting the family to concentrate their struggles in the therapy hour, getting them to begin talking to each other about their problems. He can be fairly demanding in this stage, and, if the family challenges his approach, he can and probably will respond quite strongly. The authors have never had negative results from angrily scolding a family that challenged their leadership early in the therapy process; the involvement here is real and important—belief in a personal style and approach, and determination to be effective. This assertiveness on the therapist's part is particularly valuable for the young therapist, in that it quickly produces transference in the family. The therapist is seen as an authority. Attacking the family is really appropriate only if the family, or one of its members, attacks or challenges the therapist first, and it is most effective if he shares the reasons for the anger—it matters to him that his work be effective.

Too often, however, the beginning therapist does the opposite: he avoids his anger at the family's attempt to control the therapy process, he is pseudomutual, and he attempts to reduce his anxiety about the distance between the therapeutic team and the family by becoming prematurely involved in a "warm" response to one individual in the family. This early move to individual therapy within the family context is usually damaging, in that it is dishonest and robs the family of its need to confront each other.

In the second stage, the therapist waits while the family confronts each other; he is listening and learning. The family takes up most of the hour arguing and debating with each other. The therapist interprets, deepening the level of the encounter. As the family begins to tire of their confrontation and pressure, the therapist becomes more active, helping to break up some of the stereotyped patterns as the family members achieve more individuation and thus more freedom in responding to each other. During this period the therapist's involvement with and caring for the family increases as he sees them struggle.

In the third stage, the family's despair increases: They have failed in resolving the conflicts through confrontation, and they sense for the first time the possibility of turning to the therapist for "new information"—not cognitive information, but the total information of the therapist's world. They have become interested in the therapist through his interventions during their fights, or through his sometimes surprising and paradoxical reactions to them. The essence of the third stage is the therapist's sharing his own person, allowing himself to be open and involved. But it is a very difficult moment for the therapist when the family turns to him, to the team, and says, with honest interest and considerable desperation: "How about you?" It is a difficult moment because they refer to the therapist's *person,* not his ideas or strategies.

Perhaps the most critical response is the therapist's final openness about his own caring. He looks across the room and sees a person whom he sees as like part of himself, and he feels loving toward that person and expresses that feeling. Such moments of encounter can be quietly and wonderfully powerful, and they are all the more exciting for the fact that the whole family is watching, and learning. Such a breakthrough, one therapist and one person in the family having a loving encounter, is usually followed by a series of such experiences between therapists and family members. These are the core events in family therapy.

The fourth stage might be called the "creative stage," in that the family takes the model of the therapist-family member encounter and adopts it in relating to each other. Gaining a new sense of unity in the family, they are confident enough to attack each other with more directness and more personal investment, and increased savageness may erupt in parallel with increased warmth. The therapist participates in this stage actively as a person, learning from the family, sharing many aspects of his own person. He argues with them about their own fate out of his personal investment in them.

The fifth stage is anti-climactic, alternatively social and humorous and educational, an attempt to understand the powerful events that have swept through the family. And there is an emphasis on prevention: How can they avoid getting in this dilemma again?

There is perhaps no challenge more threatening to the young or beginning family therapist than the opportunity, indeed the necessity, to be involved, to be fully a person in the therapy hour. It is difficult to express anger; it is even more difficult to express love. So often we suppress our caring, positive feelings about the family, hardly realizing that we have them. After all, this is work, not romance. We think, and plod, and miss the chance to sing. Perhaps many therapists even avoid family therapy altogether because of their embarrassment about being open about caring about their clients. Yet, for families whose self-esteem is low, whose experience of themselves is negative, there can be no more important event than someone's *experiencing them positively* and sharing that positive experience. Of course, the experience must be genuine to be helpful. And there are many other aspects of his experience that the therapist can and should share: his boredom, his anxiety, his anger, his vulgarity, his irresponsible silliness, his wit, his human condition. In openly acknowledging his emotional life of the moment, the therapist teaches, in the most intimate way, self-acceptance. This openness is particularly powerful if the therapist is free enough of pressing internal conflicts to fully participate in and respond to the family-therapist encounter. By struggling to be more fully a person in the therapy hour, the therapist models growth for the family.

The therapist's involvement with the family is most positive and most therapeutic if it is in the context of a therapeutic team that is itself warm, stimulating, and creative. The relationship between the therapists permits them to become more involved with the family with the knowledge that they have the support of an alternative relationship.

Family therapy presents a series of challenges to the intelligence, the maturity, and the humaneness of any therapist who risks trying it. The authors have outlined some of the difficulties, and the dead-end paths down which one is tempted to stray. They have probably focused too strongly on the negative. It should be clear, however, that for every challenge and pitfall, there is the possibility of exciting growth for the therapist as well as for the family.

REFERENCES

1. Bowen M: The use of family theory in clinical practice. Compr Psychiatry 7:345–374, 1966

2. Bowen M: Toward the differentiation of a self in one's own family. Unpublished

3. Jackson DD: Family rules. Arch Gen Psychiatry 12:589–595, 1965

4. Malone T: Personal communication

5. Postner RS, Guttman HA, Sigal JJ, et al: Process and outcome in conjoint family therapy. Fam Process 10:451–474, 1971

6. Reik T: Listening with the Third Ear. New York, Farrar & Straus, 1948

7. Speck RV, Reuveni V: Network therapy—A developing concept. Fam Process 8:182–191, 1969

8. Wynne LC, Ryckoff IM, Day J, et al: Pseudo-mutuality in the family relations of schizophrenics. Psychiatry 21:205–220, 1958

INDEX